*The Restless Brahmin*

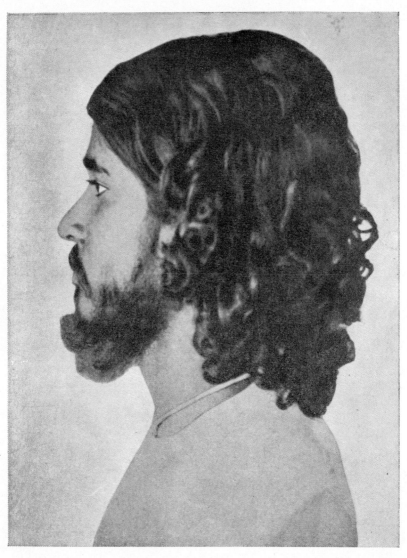

Narendranath Bhattacharya (M. N. Roy) in 1910 at the time of his arrest in the Howrah Conspiracy Case.

[ *Courtesy* : Y. B. Chavan, Minister for Home Affairs, Government of India. ]

# The Restless Brahmin

EARLY LIFE OF M. N. ROY

Samaren Roy

*To Blair*

*Samaren Roy*
*26 April 1970*

*With a foreword by*
Jadugopal Mukherjee

## ALLIED PUBLISHERS

BOMBAY CALCUTTA NEW DELHI
MADRAS BANGALORE

*First Published 1970*

**ALLIED PUBLISHERS PRIVATE LIMITED**
15 Graham Road, Ballard Estate, Bombay 1
17 Chittaranjan Avenue, Calcutta 13
13/14 Asaf Ali Road, New Delhi 1
38-C Mount Road, Madras 6
39/1 J. C. Road, Bangalore 2

© INSTITUTE OF POLITICAL AND SOCIAL STUDIES

# Foreword

THE DAY NAREN BHATTACHARYA WAS ARRESTED IN CONNECTION with the Garden Reach dacoity, a saddened Jatin Mukherjee came to my house and said: "My right arm has been broken." The Garden Reach dacoity was an act of supreme courage and daring, and it was executed by the cool-headed brain of Naren Bhattacharya in a perfect manner. Not a shot was fired. I was always opposed to dacoities, especially in Indian homes, but I approved of the Garden Reach dacoity because that was the first time the money of a British firm was looted.

We belonged to a secret society, and as such I can say about Naren Bhattacharya only what I know personally, and have direct knowledge of. In our revolutionary days, we had no right to enquire about any activity or to express our curiosity about anything in which we were not directly involved. We were inspired by the ideal of the secret society and patriotism as preached by Bankim Chandra in his novel, *Ananda Math*.

I first met Naren Bhattacharya in the Anushilan Samity about 1905 or 1906. Anushilan Samity's office at 49, Cornwallis Street had lodging arrangement for its workers, and Naren often stayed there. He and Harikumar Chakravarty became members of the Samity together.

The Anushilan Samity was started as an open society for imparting physical training to Bengali youths and inspire them with the ideals of the freedom of the Motherland. The leader of the Samity, Satish Bose, and many of the founding members of the Samity as well as Shri Hem Chandra Ghosh of Dacca were inspired by Swami Vivekananda to liberate the Motherland from the bondage of the foreign power. The influences of Swamiji and of Sister Nivedita on the development of the idea of freedom of the Motherland were profound. Even Naren and Harikumar first went to the Belur Math and then joined the Anushilan Samity.

The Anushilan Samity later developed into two wings: one secret and the other open. This was done by Pramatha Mitra, Barrister, after he joined the Samity and became its President. Pramatha Mitra joined the Samity after being approached by Satish Bose through Sashi Bhusan Roy Choudhury, a great constructive worker of Sodepur, 24-Parganas. The open wing devoted itself to social work and service, a spirit that was derived from the work of the missionaries in the Belur Math. The secret wing of the Samity was the handiwork of Pramatha Mitra who developed the secret society within Anushilan on the ideals of *Ananda Math* and also on the lines of the French revolutionaries. Pramatha Mitra acquainted himself with the French revolutionaries while studying in England.

The first propounder of the idea of achieving independence by physical force was Jatindranath Banerjee, who later became famous as Niralamba Swami. It was he who went to Baroda to take military training so that he could train Bengalis in military warfare and strategy. It was Jatindranath Banerjee who also persuaded Sri Aurobindo to join revolutionary politics in Bengal. But we regarded Jatindranath as a bigger leader. Jatindranath founded a training centre at Upper Circular Road in 1902 on his return from Baroda, which became popularly known as the East Club. Sister Nivedita was an important member of the Executive body of the Club. She gave her library of revolutionary literature to the Club.

As far as I know, Naren was first initiated into revolutionary society by Avinash Bhattacharya of Arbelia. Avinash was recruited by Jatindranath Banerjee to the East Club in 1903. Later, Naren joined the Anushilan Samity and soon became an important member. Naren first met Jatin Mukherjee (of Balasore fame) in the Anushilan Samity, but became close to Jatin Mukherjee only during the trial of the Howrah Gang Case when they were together in jail. After acquittal from the Howrah Gang Case, Naren started moving with the idea of reorganising the revolutionary party with Jatin Mukherjee as the leader. Naren became very active from then on, and urged me several times to meet Jatin Mukherjee. However, I had the feeling that if I were a worthy revolutionary Jatin Mukherjee himself would come to me. This he did after Naren's arrest in 1915.

Naren played an important role in building up the revolutionary party in 1914 with Jatin Mukherjee as the supreme leader. The revolutionary party that we had built up was a federation of the different revolutionary societies, almost all of which were in moribund state at the time. We did not give it any name. The name, Jugantar, was like the blanket description *Hindu* that our enemies, the British officers, particularly, Charles Tegart, the then D.I.G., C.I.D. (Bengal), gave it by saying all the time "Jugantar has done this, Jugantar has done that". The common link between us and the earlier Jugantar group was the name of the bulletin, that we began to publish in the name of *Jugantar* after the formation of the revolutionary party. We chose the name, *Jugantar,* because of the popularity the journal had acquired. We, however, had a much more elaborate and grandiose plan for the liberation of the country than what Barin Ghosh and the group had ever conceived of.

Naren was not very well educated. He had only passed the Entrance Examination. He later had himself educated while abroad. We rarely discussed religion in those days. Naren and I were close friends, and we discussed a lot of politics and political methods. As a follower of Mazzini, I kept religion and politics apart. Naren also followed the same line.

Although very cool-headed when it came to political action, Naren behaved in a school-masterly way with most of his colleagues. Once I took him instead of Jatin Mukherjee, who had already gone to Balasore, to a secret meeting with the Barisal group. Naren was absconding at the time, in early 1915, and I took him from his hiding place in Kidderpore. He led the discussion, but Swami Prajnanananda, leader of the Barisal group, wanted to know in greater details about our plan. Naren would not tell more than what he thought the Barisal group should know. This almost led to a virtual breakdown of the negotiations for merger of this group with our organisation for which purpose the meeting was arranged. After safely returning him to his hiding place, I resumed the discussion and the Barisal group finally joined us.

When Naren left for Batavia for the second time in late 1915, he had already smelt danger. He took with him Phani Chakravarty to work as his assistant. He did not return from the second trip until long after; and wrote to me for the first time from Moscow in early 'twenties. Arriving in USA, Naren first met my brother, Dhangopal Mukherjee, with whom he put up. Dhan was preinformed about his possible visit and had made arrangements accordingly.

Naren was one of the most colourful figures in the revolutionary movement and his organisational skill was conspicuous. Jatin Mukherjee was very much dependent upon Naren Bhattacharya and regarded him as his Second-in-Command. People know and have heard a lot about M. N. Roy, but to us Naren Bhattacharya remains a dear name. Modern students of politics should know more about that period of revolutionary movement which has already become part of history, as well as about the men who led it.

JADUGOPAL MUKHERJEE

*Ranchi (Bihar)*
*July 4, 1968*

# Preface

LALA LAJPAT RAI WROTE IN 1916: "MY EXPERIENCE OF THE
Indian revolutionaries in the U.S. has been very sad and
disappointing. . . . Their patriotism was often tainted by consideration of gain and profit . . . the only one of the Bengali
revolutionaries for whom I have had genuine respect is
M. N. Roy."[1] Jawaharlal Nehru had the same kind of respect
for Roy. In his Autobiography, he wrote: "I must say
that I was not greatly impressed by most of the Indian
political exiles that I met abroad . . . of the few I met the
only persons who impressed me intellectually were V. Chattopadhyaya and M. N. Roy." Referring to Roy, he says:
"There was a great deal of difference between us, and yet
I felt attracted towards him, . . . I was attracted to him by
his remarkable intellectual capacity."[2]

This monograph is the first part of a bigger project, a
complete biography of M. N. Roy, and deals with the early
phase of M. N. Roy's life. Besides, this book is also intended
to give a feel of the times and politics that M. N. Roy, as
Narendranath Bhattacharya, grew up in, before he became
a world figure in the company of Lenin. His former name,
Naren Bhattacharya, is used in the text of this book.

To write a complete biography of M. N. Roy, whom Lenin
regarded as "the best representative of colonial revolution-
ism"[3] is a difficult task, if only for the geographical distances
involved in his varied political life. To write about the
period of his life covered in this book is not less so in view
of the secret nature of the groups that flourished and func-
tioned in the early days of militant nationalist movement
in India. Few authors have tried to write an objective

[1] Extracts from the *Diary of Lala Lajpat Rai, 1914-1917*, now preserved
in the National Archives, Government of India, New Delhi.

[2] Jawaharlal Nehru: *An Autobiography*, London, 1936, pp. 154, 218.

[3] Fe. Borkenau: *The Communist International*, London, 1938, p. 288.

account of the militant nationalist movement that developed in Bengal between 1905 and 1916 in which Roy played a vital role. An understanding of this part of Roy's life is, however, essential for a study of man's complete life, and is in itself important for students of political history.

The period when Roy began his political activities was one when British rule had lost its liberal significance. In fact after the 1857 uprising the British Government decided merely to carry on the economic exploitation of this country and let other goals go by. Hence the Government did not attempt any major social reform after the enactment of the Widow Remarriage Bill in 1856 until the Age of Consent (Sarda) Act was promulgated in 1930. On the contrary, many of its Acts—like the Vernacular Press Act, the Universities Act of 1904 and others—were socially repressive. It was a period comparable to that of the stagnant and decaying period of Mughal rule and its major accomplishments were the building of railways, opening of coal and copper mines, several irrigation projects (all outside Bengal)—all can be viewed in terms of economic exploitation.

The Moderate leaders who had formed the Indian National Congress in 1885 failed to galvanise and enthuse the masses of India to participate in a movement for the freedom of the country from this rule of the alien exploiters. The task of transforming the nationalist movement from an "intellectual pastime" of a few into a mass movement was left to be accomplished by those known as the "Extremist" or "Militant" nationalists like, Bal Gangadhar Tilak of Maharashtra, Lala Lajpat Rai of Punjab, Bipin Chandra Pal and Aurobindo Ghosh of Bengal. These leaders rejected the policy of "prayer and petitions" of the Moderates and initiated a militant movement for complete independence based on revolutionary action, including terrorism and armed revolt, which climaxed in the abortive Indo-German plan for armed insurrection in the wake of the first world war. The militant nationalist movement drew its strength and inspiration from an intensive revivalist and religious fervour created by the writings of Bankim Chandra Chatterjee, Swami Vivekananda, and others.

"The fundamental difference between the older political agitations and the new nationalist movement", wrote Bipin Chandra Pal (1858-1932), "... is (1) its intensely spiritual and religious character ... and (2) its strong grip on the actualities of Indian life and thought as against the imitative character of the older and earlier social and political activities."[4]

Born in a priestly Brahmin family in 1887, M. N. Roy was brought up in this climate of intense religious and nationalist revival, and began his life in the quest of spiritual freedom. In this monograph, I have endeavoured to depict the inner struggles of this restless Brahmin and his transformation from a seeker of spiritual freedom to a most activist and adventurist militant nationalist and his dominant role in the formation of the Jugantar Party in 1914. This book ends with his attempt, in collaboration with Germans, to import arms for waging an armed struggle against the British rulers in the wake of the First World War and his daring missions to Batavia and other countries in South-East Asia in search of arms.

Because of the scarcity of authentic published materials, I have largely depended upon the interviews I had with many of the participants in this freedom fight who had known and collaborated with Roy. In a sense, this book can be called a story told by those great freedom fighters of the country to all of whom I remain indebted. I shall cherish those moments of interviews which have been in themselves a fascinating experience. The interviews throw a lot of significant insights into the life and thinking of these revolutionaries who had engaged themselves in one of the most difficult and pioneering political battles for the independence of the country and at some future date I hope to publish these interviews for the benefit of the students of Indian political history.

[4] Bipin Chandra Pal: *The Spirit of Indian Nationalism*, London, 1910, p. 29.

## PREFACE

I must also express my deep gratitude to my friend Tridib Ghosh who has assisted me in the collection of research materials, to Sushil Mukherjee for the use of his valuable library on M. N. Roy, to Prof. Nirupam Chatterjee for going through the manuscript and to my friends H. B. Roy and Hamdi Bey for various suggestions. I am also deeply indebted to Mr. K. K. Sinha, Director of the Institute of Political and Social Studies for his generous help and advice for the publication of the book.

SAMAREN ROY

*Calcutta*
*October* 10, 1969

# Acknowledgements

THE AUTHOR WISHES TO ACKNOWLEDGE HIS DEEP GRATITUDE TO THE FOLLOWING gentlemen who have very kindly given him their valuable time for long hours of interview:

1. *Nirvan Swami,* alias Satish Chandra Sarkar (aged 85), of Rajshahi. Swami was a close associate of Aurobindo and Barin Ghosh, Jatindranath Banerjee, Jatin Mukherjee and Naren Bhattacharya.
2. *Hem Chandra Ghosh* (*b.* 1884, in Dacca); initiated into revolutionary politics by Swami Vivekananda; founder of the Volunteers Club, Dacca and later of Bengal Volunteers.
3. *Dr. Jadugopal Mukherjee* (*b.* 1886), one of the top leaders of the Jugantar Party, was in charge of Foreign Affairs of the party; joined Anushilan Samity in 1905.
4. *Nalini Kanta Kar* (aged about 80), close associate of Jatin Mukherjee.
5. *Kali Prasad Banerjee* (aged about 78), leader of Faridpur Group.
6. *Bhupati Majumdar* (*b.* 1890), former Minister of West Bengal Government after independence; a leader of the Jugantar Party.
7. *Surendra Mohan Ghosh,* M.P., a leader of the Jugantar Party.
8. *Monoranjan Gupta,* M.L.C. (aged about 80), one of the leaders of Barisal group.
9. *Dr. Aswini Lal Roy* (aged 85), one of the earliest members of the Anushilan Samity.
10. *Amar Krishna Ghosh* (aged about 79), younger brother of Atul Krishna Ghosh, and Secretary of the Congress Legislature Party in the 'thirties.
11. *Satish Chandra Chakravarty,* mentioned in the Sedition Committee Report as the man sent for blowing up the bridge over the river Ajoy. Died on October 14, 1968 at the age of 77. One of the leaders of the Jugantar and a member of the West Bengal Legislative Assembly, 1946-51.
12. *Bhupendra Kumar Dutt* (aged 75), a leader of the Jugantar Party.
13. *Jitendra Kumar Basu* (aged about 75), nephew of Atul Krishna Ghosh.
14. *Sarat Chandra Ghosh* (died in September 1968 at the age of 80), one of the earliest members of the Anushilan Samity.
15. *Haridas Dutt* (aged about 78), associated with looting of the Mauser pistols from the Rodda and Company.
16. *Dr. Nalini Ranjan Sen Gupta* (aged 82), member of the outer circle of the Anushilan Samity.

# ACKNOWLEDGEMENTS

17. *Purna Sen* (now about 80), accused in the Alipore Bomb Case.
18. *Alok Chakravarty* (aged about 72), nephew of M. N. Roy.
19. *Kali Charan Ghosh* (aged about 76), of Changripota, author of *The Roll of Honour.*
20. *Nripen Chakravarty* (aged about 65), nephew of M. N. Roy.
21. *Lalit Mohan Bhattacharya,* younger brother of M. N. Roy.

# Contents

# Abbreviations

1. Dr. Jadugopal

Jadugopal Mukherjee: *Biplabi Jibaner Smriti* (Memoirs of revolutionary life), in Bengali. Indian Associated Publishing Co. (P) Ltd., Calcutta, 1956.

2. Harikumar

Harikumar Chakravarty: *Manabendranath Smarane* (In memory of Manabendranath), in Bengali, published by Radical Humanist Association, Calcutta, 1954.

3. *Viswa-Vivek*

Harikumar Chakravarty's article titled "Biplabi Andolane Swamijir Prabhav" (Swamiji's Influence on Revolutionary Movement) in *Viswa-Vivek: Centenary Volume on Swami Vivekananda*, published by Bak-Sahitya, Calcutta, 2nd edition, 1966.

4. B. B. Majumdar

Bimanbehari Majumdar: *Militant Nationalism in India*, General Printers and Publishers, Calcutta, 1966.

5. Prithwin Mukherjee

Prithwindranath Mukhopadhyaya: "Sadhak Biplabi Jatindranath" (Serialised biography of Jatin Mukherjee) published in *The Basumati*, Bengali Weekly, from September 9, 1965 onwards.

# Prologue

BY THE END OF THE SIXTEENTH CENTURY INDIAN SOCIETY WAS pervaded by an acute sense of frustration and demoralisation. Corruption, inefficiency and court intrigues of the decaying Muslim rule, which caused ruin of their empire, gave rise not only to a general unrest but also to incredible poverty and hardship among the people and consequent social insecurity. The sixteenth century Bengali poetess, Chandravati, gave a first-hand account of the situation in her famous ballad on the robber chief, Kenaram. The tale which she unfolds is that of a "land racked with and riven by anarchy, of deserted homesteads, and of a people harried and panic-stricken under a chaotic administration". Aurangzeb's long rule from 1658 to 1707 was both the culminating point of the Mughal empire as well as the beginning of its decay. None of Aurangzeb's successors was any better than a puppet and almost all of them were devoid of integrity, character, imagination and administrative ability. It was at such a time that the British established their rule in India.

The contact with the West opened up a new chapter in India's history, and instilled new vitality. By the time the British came to India, Europe had undergone a major revolution in her own life and thought. The subsequent spread of English education and the opening up of new economic and employment opportunities created a new social force in Bengal where the English established their rule first.

1

A

Describing the situation, Sir Jadunath Sarkar wrote: "In our hopelessly decadent society the rational progressive spirit of Europe struck with irresistible force. First of all, an honest and efficient administration was imposed on the country...to ensure peace and economic growth. Then, within one generation, the land began to recover from the plight of medieval theocratic rule.... The dry bones of a stationary, oriental society began to stir under the wand of a heaven-sent magician. It was truly a renaissance, wider, deeper and more revolutionary than that of Europe after the fall of Constantinople."[1]

With the spread of English education, a new generation emerged having access to wider reaches of knowledge. Growing sections of people began to feel the limitations and backwardness of a static society and endeavoured to carry on the movement for liberation from the bonds of ritualism, tradition and blind faith. The new social leadership that grew was helped by their access to an alternative mode of living free from the traditional feudal-patriarchal society. Thus began an era of new urges and new awakening; the old social order began to disintegrate.

At the beginning of the nineteenth century, for the first time in the history of India, the basic foundations of the orthodox social order were challenged. Rammohun Roy (1772-1833) began the movement for a new social outlook and preached a new religion abolishing caste hierarchy and meaningless rituals. He based his new religion, *Brahmoism,* on the teachings of the *Upanishads,* India's own and older philosophy, buried for centuries under the dust of ritualism and superstitions, and thereby incurred the wrath of the Brahmins and orthodox Hindus who had grown to fear change and freedom from tradition and blind faith. Thus, Rammohun ushered in a new era—the 'Young Bengal' defying tradition, and breathed new life into a dying people.

The nineteenth century became an age of creativity in Bengal under Rammohun's impact, and gave rise to fresh and healthier tensions between the bold advocates of modernism and the new and more competent defenders of orthodoxy. The defenders of orthodoxy had to resuscitate the older philosophies and teachings of India, forgotten for centuries, and equip themselves more ably against the new challenges.

In the middle of the nineteenth century however a great Brahmin demonstrated to 'Young Bengal' that ancient Indian ideas were not merely a bunch of rituals and superstitions. This man, Pundit Iswar Chandra Vidyasagar (1820-1891), brought fresh hopes and ushered in a new era of enlightenment. Vidyasagar shook the entire society and made great efforts to free people's outlook and thinking from the shackles of blind faith and superstitions, resurrecting the true spirit of ancient Indian culture and reviving ancient Indian studies. He stirred the Brahmanic hierarchy to a new sense of awakening, instilled new urges and began a new movement of education through the medium of vernacular and Sanskrit languages. The stirring was so intense that when in 1857 the sepoy mutiny broke out in Calcutta it failed to evoke any response from educated Bengalis who were more seriously engaged in the new social and educational movement.

The impact of Vidyasagar's cultural-educational movement climaxed in Michael Madhusudan Dutta's (1824-1873) penitent return to his 'native' language and moorings. Madhusudan's great poem, "Lamentations", published in the *Tattva-bodhini Patrika* in 1861 epitomises the emotional return of a prodigal son to his mother language and marks the turning point in nationalist, educational and cultural resurgence that began in the 'fifties of the nineteenth century and of which Pundit Iswar Chandra Vidyasagar can be rightfully called the chief architect.

Although still in its embryonic stage, nationalist feelings began to grow under the impact of this new literary movement in the 'sixties of the last century. The new researches of Indologists like Sir William Jones, Max Müller, Colebrook, Wilson, Cunningham, Raja Rajendralal Mitra and many others helped the growth of the new pride about India's 'glorious' past. In 1858, Pundit Dwarkanath Vidyabhusan began to publish the Bengali newspaper, *Som Prakasa,* under

3

the inspiration of Vidyasagar, providing further impetus to nationalist urges. However, it took another generation of Indians to arouse in the people the urge for active participation in the government of the country. The realisation that the government of an alien power impeded the full development of the individual and the fulfilment of the urges of the subject people began to grow in the sixties. The injustice that was done against Surendranath Banerjea (1948-1926) by the British Government by his dismissal from the Indian Civil Service because he was a 'native', the subsequent denial of his right to join the Bar and Banerjea's campaign against the injustices of the alien rulers gave rise to a new sense of national awakening that Indians had not known before.

However, the turning point in the growth of nationalist feeling was the transfer of India from the East India Company's rule to the British Crown in the wake of the 1857 uprising, although the uprising itself had failed to evoke any support from the Bengali intelligentsia. Criticising the transfer, Harish Chandra Mukherjee, editor of *Hindu Patriot* wrote: "Can a revolution in the Indian Government be authorised by (British) Parliament without consulting the wishes of the vast millions of men for whose benefit it is proposed to be made?"[2] Also in the wake of the 1857 uprising took place the famous revolt of the Indian cultivators which immensely agitated the minds of the educated Bengalis and helped the growth of nationalist feeling in Bengal.[3]

Nationalist feelings subsequently developed in two different directions: one led by the western-educated liberal politicians who stressed the importance of the development of Indian nationhood and urged larger participation of Indians in the government of the country. They welcomed the British Government and accepted the 'civilising' aspect of British rule.

Simultaneously also developed a different concept of nationalism, based upon the orthodoxy of Hinduism, chauvinistic in character. In 1861 Rajnarain Bose (1826-1899), one of the early exponents of Hindu nationalism, published the prospectus of the "Society for the Promotion of National Feelings" and later formed the first secret revolutionary society along with Sivanath Sastri.[4] In 1866, Rajnarain Bose also founded the Society for the Promotion of National Feeling to uphold Hindu cultural heritage against the onslaught of Western culture and civilisation. In 1867, Nabagopal Mitra, inspired by Rajnarain Bose, founded the *Jatiya mela* (lit: National Fair; also known as Hindu mela) giving expression to the growing yearning of the educated youth for nationalism.

However, it dawned upon Bankim Chandra Chatterjee (1838-1894) for the first time that the idea of nationalism that was developing was "an exotic plant transplanted to the Indian soil from Europe".[5] He raised nationalism to the dignity of a religion. In his masterpiece of philosophical satire, *Kamalakanter Daptar* (Diaries of Kamalakanta), Bankim identified goddess *Durga* with *Bangabhumi* (Bengal). He then went a step further and called the Motherland, the Mother and the Goddess.[6] The concrete image of the Motherland was vividly drawn by Bankim in his song, *Bande Mataram* (Hail to Thee, Oh Mother) which was later incorporated in his novel, *Ananda Math,* published in 1880. The new nationalism, which *Bande Mataram* preached, was "not a mere civic or economic or political ideal. It is a religion", said Bipin Chandra Pal, one of the high priests of militant nationalism in Bengal.

*Ananda Math* was based on the rebellion of the *sanyasis* (monks) in 1772-74 against the East India Company. Bhavananda, a leader of the *sanyasis,* explains to Mahendra, a new recruit, that the new order of *Sanyasis* does not recognise any mother but the mother country. The *sanyasis* appear in the novel under the title of the children—the children of the motherland, which is identified with the great goddess in her many manifestations, *Jagaddhatri, Kali, Durga.*

Mahendra is then taken to the different temples of the *Ananda Math* (The Temple of Bliss) by the venerable ascetic, Satyananda, and shown different images. He is first shown *Jagaddhatri* and is told to perceive in her the "Mother as She was". Next he is taken to the dark chamber

5

where he sees a fearsome figure, and he is told that this is the "Mother as She is today". In the last shrine he is shown a female figure more glorious than *Lakshmi* (Goddess of Wealth) or *Saraswati* (Goddess of Learning), in whose company she is seated, to whom the whole universe is depicted as paying homage. This, he is told, is the "Mother as She would be". Mahendra is greatly moved at the sight of the goddess *Durga,* the "Mother as She would be", and asks when they will see the Mother in this glorious form; and he is told "when all the children of the Mother learn to call her so". On his return, Satyananda has a long talk with Mahendra and initiates him into the Society of the Children. Mahendra is then taken to the temple of the "Mother as She would be" where he takes the vow of the children: "to renounce the family and riches, conquer all passions and never even to share a seat with a woman, to fight for the true religion, and as children of one mother to give up caste". Then they sing the hymn to the Mother, *"Bande Mataram"*.[7] Later, in the Anushilan Samity, the terrorist revolutionaries adopted a similar vow for their recruits.

Bankim gives an original interpretation of the goddess Kali. According to him, "Kali is the symbol of degradation of India. She is black in colour because of the intense misery of the country. She is naked, because India has been denuded of all her wealth. She wears the garland of human skulls because the whole country has become a vast burial ground. She has Siva under her feet to show that the Indians are trampling down their own welfare. He explains the image of Durga as the realisation of the future greatness of India. The mother country would call her mother."[8]

Lord Ronaldshay, who came to Bengal as the Governor of the province in 1916, wrote: "When the English came to Bengal the people of the land were decadent. They were a people whose vital spark had burned low, whose Religion of Power had become a mockery of its former self—had lost its soul of beneficence in the repetition of empty formulae and the observance of meaningless mummeries....And so it happened to them as it happens to all the weak. From pure inaction they had accepted the English Government, and with that the English race—their culture, their civilisation and their luxury. But the time had come when they must cast off the spell which had lain upon them. Already prophets of the race had arisen who had kindled once again the fires on the ancient altars. Bankim had come and had set the image of the mother in the Motherland."[9]

The principal cause of the anarchy, confusion and disintegration of the eighteenth century was the total absence of patriotic feeling and political consciousness among the people. Unstable governments, intrigues, revolts, conspiracies and assassinations became so common between the last days of Mughal rule and the advent of the British that people lost all interest and faith in the government of the country. Thousands of people who witnessed the Battle of Plassey (1757), according to Clive's testament, did not even throw a stone in anger or protest. That had paved the way for foreign domination.

The development of patriotic feelings and nationalist urges synchronised with the period of British rule when it lost its liberating ideas. This period, which began with the transfer in 1857 of Indian empire from the East India Company to the British Crown, saw the rapid growth of political consciousness and the assertion of nationalist sentiment. After the enactment of Widow Remarriage Bill in 1856 the British Government did not also attempt any social reform until Age of Consent (Sarda) Act of 1930. It was a stagnant period comparable to that of the later decaying Mughal rule and all that the British were interested was economic exploitation of the country. Subsequently, "the reactionary administration of Lord Lytton had roused the public from its attitude of indifference and had given a stimulus to public life". The repressive Arms Act and the Vernacular Press Act of 1878, the diversion of famine fund to the Afghan war, the Ilbert Bill controversy of 1882, the Calcutta Municipality Act, the Universities Act of 1904— all helped to stir people's anger against the alien rulers.

By 1896 the Indian National Congress was practically divided between the Moderates and the Extremists. This latter trend of thought developed in Bengal, Maharashtra and the Punjab under the leadership of the Lal-Bal-Pal group. They contended that "a good government was no substitute for self-government" and urged militant agitation against foreign rule—in opposition to the Moderates.

The earliest symptoms of dissatisfaction with the political methods of prayer and petition practised by the moderate leaders of the Indian National Congress are to be found in the series of articles written by Aurobindo Ghosh in the *Induprakash* in 1893-94. Aurobindo was influenced by the new militant type of nationalism that had developed in Maharashtra at this time.

Swami Vivekananda (1863-1902) gave the vital spark that was needed to revitalise the nation at this stage. On his 'triumphant' return from a tour of the Western countries in 1897, Vivekananda declared at Kumbakonam: "What our country now wants are the muscles of iron and nerves of steel, gigantic will which nothing can resist."[10] Vivekananda drew upon the Vedantic philosophy as well as the *Gita* to instil courage and strength in the people. Explaining the message of the *Gita,* he wrote: "The weak have no place here, in this life or in the other life. Weakness leads to slavery, weakness is death." It was Vivekananda who gave to the Bengali mind the idea of a great nation; he gave life and meaning to the cult of the Motherland preached by Bankim Chandra in his *Ananda Math.* The revolutionary movement that began in Bengal at the turn of the century was inspired by Vivekananda's exhortation to forsake weakness and was based on the organisation of secret societies and armed revolt on the lines of the *sanyasi* rebellion as depicted in Bankim Chandra's *Ananda Math.*

The seeds of the new spirit, of nationalism and revolution, having been sown, began to sprout and attract people. It first dawned upon Jatindranath Banerjee (later known as Niralamba Swami) to give practical shape to the idea of applying force for the liberation of the Motherland and to train Bengalis in the use of arms for political purposes. With that mission he went to Baroda in 1899 with an introduction to Aurobindo Ghose.[11] After his failure in the ICS Examination, Aurobindo (1872-1950) returned to India and joined the Educational Service of the Maharaja of Baroda and became the Vice-Principal of the Gaekwad College. Aurobindo was a great favourite of the Maharaja of Baroda and Jatindranath entered the army of the Maharaja with the help of Aurobindo. As Bengalis were denied entry into military services, Jatindranath joined the army adopting the surname, Upadhyaya, in order to evade the suspicion of the British police.

Jatindranath returned to Calcutta in 1902 and set up a training centre where he combined physical culture with education in revolutionary nationalism. He rented a house at 108, Upper Circular Road, close to the Sukea Street Police Station, and lived there with his wife so as to cause least suspicion to the police. Vivekananda's ablest disciple, Sister Nivedita, encouraged Jatindranath in his mission and helped him set up a library for revolutionaries by donating about 200 books from her own and became an Executive Member of Jatindranath's East Club. It was Sister Nivedita who urged upon Indians to work for the liberation of the country instead of pursuing the ideal of spiritual *'moksha'* (liberation).

In Calcutta and other towns of Bengal, physical culture centres, where wrestling and *lathi* play were taught, had by then become popular and fashionable among young men of the educated and well-to-do families, the *bhadralok* class. The revolutionaries resorted to *lathi* play and wrestling because in the first place being traditional forms of physical culture they would cause least suspicion to the government and second, rigorous enforcement of arms control in Bengal had left them with those two modes as the only outlets for exercises in violence. The *Anushilan Samity* (Society for the Promotion of Culture) was founded as such a centre for physical culture and moral training with strong nationalist bias by Satish Chandra Bose in 1902. The name *'anushilan'* (training in mental and moral upliftment) was taken from Bankim Chandra's book, *Dharma Tattva* in which the subject, *anushilan,* was discussed. According to Bankim, *Anushilan* is fulfilment and integration of all human faculties—

9

physical, intellectual, active and creative—and through dedication of this unified, pure, full-blown and self-controlled personality to the good of the world.[12] The Anushilan Samity had earlier received inspiration from Vivekananda. Most of the founding members of the Samity used to visit Vivekananda at the Belur *Math* and had been inspired by him in revolutionary nationalism. One of the Swamis (monks) of the Belur *Math,* Swami Saradananda, later took classes on the *Gita* at the Anushilan Samity. The Hindu monastic orders played a not-too-insignificant role in the spread of the idea of revolutionary nationalism. The holding of the *Gita* classes at the Anushilan Samity is only one such illustration. There were strong links between other monastic orders and personal 'gurus' with most of the revolutionary leaders of the time which provided a strong religious-spiritual overtone to the early militant nationalist movement.

Soon after Jatindranath had started his centre at the Upper Circular Road residence, Aurobindo visited Calcutta accompanied by his brother, Barin, to develop the centre and build up the revolutionary movement in Bengal. Disappointed at the lack of revolutionary fervour of the Bengalis and personal rivalries among different leaders of Bengal,[13] Aurobindo decided to return to Baroda a few months later leaving Barin behind. Aurobindo, however, came back to Bengal in 1903 to resolve the differences that soon developed between Barin and Jatindranath, and stayed at the residence of Jogendranath Vidyabhusan. While staying at the residence of Jogendranath Vidyabhusan (who rendered into Bengali the lives of Garibaldi and Mazzini which became handbooks for Bengali revolutionaries), Jatin Mukherjee met him and became his revolutionary disciple. About this time Pramatha Mitra, later President of the Anushilan Samity, arranged a meeting between the Baroda group of Aurobindo, Barin and Jatindranath Banerjee and the leaders of the Anushilan Samity, and the two groups merged into a single organisation with Pramatha Mitra as the President, Aurobindo and C. R. Das as Vice-Presidents and Suren Tagore as Treasurer. Pramatha Mitra realised that in order to build up a strong movement for independence—a well-knit organised militant party was necessary which would have both an open wing to serve as the platform and a secret wing with active militant fighters for freedom. The open wing would serve as the recruitment centre and the trained cadres would then work in the secret wing. He realised that in order to implement this idea it was necessary to unite all available human materials scattered in different groups and he prevailed upon the two major groups to unite with this idea.

Following the merger, the Anushilan Samity became the first such united revolutionary political group in Bengal and it soon acted as the platform for all revolutionaries.

Aurobindo, however, returned to Baroda and came back to Bengal in the wake of the British decision to partition the province of Bengal in 1905. Soon after, he gave up his Baroda job to take up the leadership of the revolutionary movement in Bengal. About this time he wrote the pamphlet, *Bhawani Mandir* (The Temple of Bhawani) which set out the aims and the objects of the revolutionaries and exhorted its readers to invoke the blessings of *Sakti* so that they might become true soldiers in the fight for freedom.

A large number of physical culture centres, *samities* and *ashramas,* had grown up in different parts of Bengal at the time of partition. The *samities* took up different names in different places, as for instance, the Atmonnati Samity in Bowbazar (Calcutta), the Bandhav Samity of Barisal, the Suhrid and Sadhana Samities in Mymensingh, Brati Samity in Khulna and Faridpur, but the object was the same, *anushilan.* They became centres of revolutionary activity and were later banned by the government. All these samities were formed by individual leaders with rigid discipline because they had to function secretly in view of strict governmental watch. However, the Anushilan Samity remained the broad platform for all the revolutionaries and the revolutionary societies.

At the height of the anti-partition agitation in Bengal towards the latter part of 1905, differences arose between Pramatha Mitra and Barin Ghose as to the methods and

11

tactics of revolution. Pramatha Mitra believed that it was necessary to organise a well-knit party with extensive organisational bases throughout the State before any militant action was precipitated. Barin, however, believed that militant action would help stir up the Bengalis from their existing attitude of resignation and passivity and develop an urge for independence and hatred of the British rulers. A general meeting of the All Bengal Revolutionary Societies was, therefore, called in 1906 at the residence of Raja Subodh Chandra Mullick where the differences were temporarily resolved. However, Barin soon decided to found a party of his own to organise the rebellion against the government because he felt that the time was ripe for such an uprising. With that object and also in order to arouse revolutionary spirit, Barin started the journal, *Jugantar,* in March 1906 with Avinash Chandra Bhattacharya (the Arbelia cousin of M. N. Roy) and Bhupendranath Dutt (younger brother of Swami Vivekananda) as his associates. In the same year, Aurobindo also took up a teaching job in the newly-started National College in Calcutta, giving up his job in Baroda, and in November, started the journal, *Bande Mataram,* in English language, with Subodh Mullick, Shyam Sundar Chakravarty and Bipin Pal as his collaborators.

The group which later formed around the journal, *Jugantar,* came to be loosely called the Jugantar group and were known as the extremists among the revolutionary groups; and it soon became the chief centre of the younger generation and the students.

The revolutionary fervour that was produced in Bengal under the impact of Bankim Chandra and Vivekananda and the leadership of Aurobindo made its dramatic impact at the annual session of the Indian National Congress held in Benares in 1905. It was at this session that Sister Nivedita, the Irish lady who became a disciple of Swami Vivekananda, made an impassioned plea for struggle for India's independence and the session was opened with the *Bande Mataram* song. At this session a new group led by Lala Lajpat Rai urged change in the political method of the Congress towards greater militancy. This eventually resulted in the split within the Congress in 1907 at its Surat Session with the expulsion of the advocates of militant nationalism, dubbed as the Lal-Bal-Pal group.

The extremist group which came to be known as the Lal-Bal-Pal group was formed at the Calcutta session of the Congress in 1906. At this session Aurobindo pursuaded the Bengal group to accept Tilak as the leader of this group. As a matter of fact, the Calcutta Congress anticipated Surat. "While Lajpat Rai belonged to the extreme right of this new faction, Pal stood at the centre after his quarrel with Aurobindo's group over the latter's support of swadeshi (nationalist) dacoities and terrorist outrages."[14]

Aurobindo was on the far left. He not only took over the editorship of the *Bande Mataram* from Bipin Pal but fully cooperated with the programme of his brother, Barin Ghosh, as preached through the *Jugantar*. Hemchandra Kanungo, an associate of Aurobindo and Barin and an accused in the Alipore Bomb Case, associates Aurobindo with the Jugantar group's programme from the beginning, e.g. with attempts on Bampfylde Fuller's life, swadeshi dacoities and the propagation of terrorist ideas.[15]

Aurobindo welcomed the split at Surat as "God's will" and had already thought of setting up a central revolutionary body—a sort of parallel government. In *Aurobindo on Himself and on the Mother,* published long afterwards, "Aurobindo admits that he had been intimately connected with organizing revolutionary activities as a preparation for open revolt, in case passive resistance proved insufficient for the purpose".[16]

The subsequent political movement in Bengal was dominated by the revolutionaries functioning through the different secret societies until the formation of the Jugantar Party on the eve of the first world war, which, under the leadership of Jatin Mukherjee and able assistance of M. N. Roy organised the abortive armed insurrection against the British rule in India in 1915.

## NOTES AND REFERENCES

[1] Sir Jadunath Sarkar: *Fall of the Mughal Empire,* Vol. IV.

[2] Quoted from Nemai Sadhan Bose: *Indian Awakening and Bengal* (Firma K. L. Mukhopadhyaya, Calcutta, 1960), pp. 164-65.

[3] *Ibid.*: p. 165. See also Blair Kling: *The Blue Mutiny.*

[4] B. B. Majumdar: *History of Political Thought,* Vol. I, Bengal, University of Calcutta, 1934, p. 241.

[5] *Ibid.*: p. 413.

[6] *Ibid.*: pp. 417-18.

[7] Lord Ronaldshay: *The Heart of Aryavarta,* pp. 108-09.

[8] B. B. Majumdar: *History of Political Thought,* Bengal, p. 422.

[9] Lord Ronaldshay: *The Heart of Aryavarta,* p. 99.

[10] Quoted from B. B. Majumdar: *Militant Nationalism in India,* p. 18.

[11] Barindra Kumar Ghosh: *Agni-Yuga* (Revolutionary Age), Book Corporation Ltd., Calcutta, 1948, p. 33.

[12] Dr Amales Tripathi: *The Extremist Challenge,* Orient Longmans, Calcutta, p. 13.

[13] Barin Ghosh: *Agni-Yuga* (Revolutionary Age), p. 112.

[14] Amales Tripathi: *The Extremist Challenge,* p. 124.

[15] Hemchandra Kanungo: *Banglay Biplab Prachesta,* pp. 118-48.

[16] Amales Tripathi: *The Extremist Challenge,* p. 135.

# I. Journey to Changripota

THE FIRST WORLD WAR BROKE OUT ON 4TH AUGUST 1914. SOON after, on a rainy, dark and desolate evening, a 6′ 2″ tall, dark, thin, dhoti-clad Bengali met the German Consul-General in Calcutta. With hopes of a long-cherished ambition fulfilled, he discussed with the Consul-General the plan for arms aid to Indian revolutionaries to drive the British out of India. A series of meetings and negotiations followed.

This man, Narendranath Bhattacharya (alias M. N. Roy), had then Jatin Mukherji brought back to Calcutta. At a secret meeting of the different revolutionary groups of Bengal, Jatin Mukherji was then elected the Commander-in-Chief of the revolutionary forces in India, and he soon joined in the discussion with the Germans. Another round of meetings followed to give final shape to the plan.

On 20th December 1914, the German Consul-General in Calcutta informed Berlin that "the activities of the secret revolutionary societies (were) very significant, especially those of Bengal" and suggested that his "Government should avail itself of this opportunity of undermining British power and should help these revolutionaries actively".[1]

The Germans then asked the Bengal Revolutionary Group to send a representative to Batavia to negotiate with the Germans there to finalise the plans for the arms aid. Accordingly, Naren Bhattacharya, the chief architect of the plan, was sent to Batavia in April 1915 as the representative of the revolutionary groups.

Another political drama was being enacted elsewhere in India simultaneously. In December 1914, the Indian National Congress met in its annual session at Madras. A special guest arrived, and everybody gave him a standing ovation. The honoured guest was Lord Pentland, then Governor of Madras. In that session Surendranath Banerjea moved a resolution "affirming loyalty of India to the British Crown".[2]

Mahatma Gandhi had then just arrived from South Africa. Shortly after the Madras session of the Congress, Mohandas Karamchand Gandhi got himself busy recruiting Indians for the British Indian army when Narendranath Bhattacharya had left for Batavia to finalise the plan for liberating India from British rule.

[Narendranath Bhattacharya (alias M. N. Roy) adopted the name, Manabendra Nath Roy (M. N. Roy) on his arrival in the United States of America in the summer of 1916, after the abortive attempt to liberate India with German help and an extensive search for arms throughout Southeast Asia. For the purpose of this book, which ends with his arrival in America and adoption of his new name, the original name, Narendranath Bhattacharya, or the abbreviated form, Naren, is used.]

Narendranath Bhattacharya was born in a priestly family. His father, Dinabandhu Bhattacharya, was the last in the line of high priests in the temple of the goddess, *Ksheputeswari,* in the village, *Ksheput,* in Midnapur District in Southwest Bengal. According to the legendary will of the goddess, revealed to the founder of the family in the prehistoric *satya yuga,* only the eldest of his direct descendants was entitled to occupy the seat in front of the goddess. The disruption of the family began when Dinabandhu left the village leaving behind his nine brothers and a sister. He continued visiting the ancestral home once a year to act as the high priest and used to depute someone to act during his absence.

Narrating the story of the goddess and the high position the temple occupies in the life of the orthodox Hindus, Naren later wrote the following legend:

"Once upon a time, in the annals of the gods, *Sakti* (Cosmic energy) was incarnated as the daughter of a king. The fair *Sati* (lit: the chaste wife) was naturally a devotee of Siva, incarnation of the universal male principle, the God of Gods, a grand ascetic, who, dressed in tiger skin, drunk with absolute detachment, strode through the land of the dead, riding on a bull, a retinue of ghosts dancing around him. Though absolutely unattached to anything in heaven and earth, the *Mahadeva* (God of Gods) could not resist the attraction of the universal female principle incarnated as *Sati*. Responding to the *tapasya* (meditation) of *Sati*, *Siva* presented himself in the court of her father. His grotesque outfit and bizarre company naturally scandalised the king. If his daughter had the incredibly bad taste of marrying the vagabond who wore a garland of snakes, he would never see her face. The mutual attraction of cosmic principles defied the wrath of an earthly king. *Sati* turned her back on the life of luxury and followed *Siva* to his ghostly haunts.

"Infuriated by the experience, the king resolved to avenge his humiliation. He invited all the Brahmins of the world to perform a great *Yajna* (large-scale ritual as prescribed in the vedas). The gods of heaven were also invited to partake of the gargantuan feast. The only exception was the God of Gods. The drunken chief of ghosts had enticed the fair daughter of the king. He must be insulted. *Siva* was sublimely indifferent to the meanness of men and pettiness of Gods. But the tender heart of *Sati* bled with pain. She would go to entreat her royal father to relent. . . .

"Sati was received not with the affection of a relenting father, but with abuse for having gone with one who lived in the graveyard. Her delicate soul withered under the fierce blast of insult hurled at the Cosmic Goodness (meaning of the word, *Siva*). At this juncture, *Siva* appeared on the scene, drunk not with detachment, but with sorrow for the death of his beloved. . . . He took the dead body of the beloved in her arms, maddened by grief, held it aloft on the points of his trident, and danced the Dionysian dance which shook heaven and earth.

"Torn by the centrifugal pull of the cosmic force, the limbs of the body flew in all direction. There were fifty-two of them, each dropped in a place which was subsequently sanctified. Pious Hindus must visit all the fifty-two places of pilgrimage. A small finger of *Sati* fell at the place where the temple of our ancestral goddess (*Ksheputeswari*) stood. The holy relic was placed in a jewel box, which was buried under the seat of the High Priest."[3]

Leaving the family's priestly vocation and the fortunes of the vast estates of the goddess in the village in Midnapur, Dinabandhu took up a teaching job, as the Head Pundit (Chief Instructor of Sanskrit) in a school in Arbelia, a village in the eastern part of the District of 24 Parganas on the east of Calcutta. After the death of his first wife he married for the second time in a family of high caste Brahmins of Changripota in southern 24 Parganas District in 1872. His fourth child—second by his second wife—Narendranath Bhattacharya, was born in Arbelia on 22nd February 1887.[4]

Dinabandhu later moved to Changripota, the village his second wife came from, about 12 miles south of Calcutta in the same District of 24 Parganas, in the year 1899.[5] Dinabandhu wanted to pass the last days of his life near the old bed of the sacred river, Ganges. The old, now dried up, bed of the river Ganges, passed through the area. With that idea Dinabandhu had been giving money to his father-in-law from time to time, and his father-in-law, who had no male child, transferred the property to him.[6]

NOTES AND REFERENCES

[1] Photostat copy of this telegram is part of the microfilmed record of the German Foreign Office now available at the National Archives, Government of India, New Delhi, and has been quoted in Prithwin Mukherjee's serialised biography of Jatin Mukherjee in *Basumati* (Weekly), (9th September 1965 to 24th February 1966).

[2] K. P. S. Menon: *Autobiography*, p. 44.

[3] "Disintegration of a Priestly Family" by M. N. Roy, published in *Radical Humanist*, dated 7th February 1954.

[4] According to the diary of Dinabandhu Bhattacharya shown to me by Lalit Bhattacharya, younger brother of Narendranath Bhattacharya (alias M. N. Roy).

[5] Interview with Lalit Bhattacharya.

[6] *Ibid.*

# II. The Formative Years

CHANGRIPOTA PROVIDED YOUNG NAREN WITH NEW IDEAS AND new friends. Here he became friendly with his elder cousin, Harikumar Chakravarty, who remained his lifelong friend and political associate, and others, many of whom sacrificed their lives in the cause of the country's freedom, including Satcori Banerjee,[1] Saileswar Bose[2] and his brother Shyam Sundar.

The group of villages, Changripota, Kodalia, Harinavi and Rajpur, was fervent with new ideas and social movements. Here were born many of the religious and social reformers of nineteenth century Bengal, notable among them, Rajnarain Bose (maternal grandfather of Aurobindo and Barin), Dwarkanath Vidyabhusan, the famous editor of *Som Prakasa* and associate of Pundit Iswar Chandra Vidyasagar, and his nephew Pundit Sivanath Sastri. Sivanath Sastri, a great scholar of the nineteenth century, tore off his Brahmanic sacred thread, to adopt the new religion, Brahmoism. He was an uncle of Naren's mother and had perceptible influence on the younger members of the family. Rajnarain Bose and Sivanath Sastri had made the first attempt at founding a secret revolutionary society in late nineteenth century and had inspired Nabagopal Mitra's *Jatiya Mela*.

Another man who wielded influence on young Naren was the former Brahmo Head Master of the local School, Umesh Dutta. Naren revived the library which Dutta had founded

19

in memory of Dwarkanath Vidyabhusan and actively engaged himself in social and intellectual work through the library.[3]

The Bose's Circus, which was very popular when Naren was young, had inspired Naren and his friends to develop their physical strength. Swami Vivekananda had said about Bose's Circus that "Moti (Bose) has shown what Bengalis can demonstrate by physical strength".[4]

"Young Naren", tells Harikumar Chakravarty, "was adventure-loving" when he first came to know him in 1899. He loved to walk long distances and wander about from orchard to orchard.[5] He loved adventure and adventure stories, but he was also constantly searching for something distant, something beyond, all the time. Naren spent lots of nights in the cremation ground looking out for ghosts,[6] and the cremation ground became one of his favourite spots for the secret meetings of his revolutionary group in later days.

Love for adventure and quest for the unknown made him restless. He often walked all the way from Changripota to Belur *Math,* founded by Swami Vivekananda, a distance of about 30 miles[7] and started visiting *ashramas* and *maths* in his quest for knowledge and truth. He also began to study Sanskrit from his father at an early age and take interest in the ancient Indian philosophies.[8]

Sometime in 1901, Naren met Sivnarain Swami, who had his *ashram* in South Calcutta and a branch in Kodalia. Reputedly a fugitive from the abortive Sepoy Mutiny of 1857, Sivnarain Swami believed that Hindu society had gone down because of caste divisions and many other ills it had imbibed through centuries of stagnation. He tried to find out men whom he could train in the true spirit of Hinduism devoid of its ills so that they could resurrect the society and usher in true freedom. He was impressed by Naren's dedication and gave him lessons in *yoga* as well as revolutionary politics. Naren also learned *lathi* play from Sivnarain Swami.[9] The yearning of young Naren to unravel the mysteries of nature went on increasing and he continued his lessons from Sivnarain Swami who was a worshipper of the Sun and stood against social discrimination. Naren told Harikumar one day "the Sun is the giver of all energies and force, and I want to know what this primal force is".[10]

While at Arbelia, Naren had read about the Chapekar brothers of Poona who had formed a society for physical and military training called "Society for the Removal of Obstacles to the Hindu religion". Naren repeatedly asked Sivnarain Swami about the Chapekar brothers and Tilak, who was charged for sedition already in 1897. Inspired by Naren's interest in revolutionary politics, Sivnarain Swami gave him lessons in nationalism and revolution, and instilled in him the urge to liberate the country from foreign rule as well as to free men from superstitious bondages.[11] Sivnarain Swami explained to him the teachings of the *Gita* not to look for success when striving for something great, nor to bother about the means when the objective was great.

Yet the soul of the restless child was not satisfied. He went from one *sadhu* to another, from one *ashram* to another, while practising *yoga* and physical culture. It was during this quest for knowledge and truth that Naren came to know the famous *Vaishnava Sadhu* of the time, Ramdas Babaji, and began taking lessons and guidance from him. Ramdas Babaji was so impressed by young Naren's dedication and quest for truth and knowledge that he wanted to make him his disciple[12] and a *sanyasi*.

But Naren's quest continued. He was not a mere religious seeker, his mind was groping for things more real and he wanted to do something. He wanted freedom. One night in 1904 during this early quest for truth and freedom, Naren told Harikumar and Saileswar,[13] "we have to do something".[14] The three friends decided to leave their homes before sunrise next morning[15] to find out the true path and meaning of freedom.

In this trip Naren went to Arbelia where he met his elder cousin, Avinash Bhattacharya. Avinash had already joined the revolutionary centre, East Club, at 108 Circular Road, founded by Jatindranath Banerjee. Avinash gave him political ideas—the country's call for the formation of revolutionary centres and introduced Naren to Barin Ghosh. On his return Naren called his friends and organised such a centre at Changripota which later came to be known as the Changripota group. This group, in later days, became a strong base of Jatin Mukherjee[16] and played a most vital role in the organisation of the Jugantar Party.

Naren's conception of freedom was more spiritualistic than political until then. His transformation into revolutionary nationalism happened later—in the wake of the anti-partition agitation in Bengal; but throughout his life the basic spiritual foundation of the concept of freedom remained imbedded in him. In the prime of his life, addressing the Second All India Political Study Camp of the Radical Democratic Party at Dehra Dun, 6th-18th May 1946, Naren, then M. N. Roy, said: "When as a school boy of fourteen, I began my political life, which may end in nothing, I wanted to be free. Independence, absolute and complete, is a new-fangled idea. The old-fashioned revolutionaries thought in terms of freedom. In those days we had not read Marx. We did not know about the existence of the proletariat. Still many had spent their lives in jail and went to the gallows. There was no proletariat to propel them. They were not conscious of class struggle. They did not know exactly how those conditions could be changed. But they tried to change them, anyhow. I began my political life with that spirit, and I still draw my inspiration rather from that spirit than from the three volumes of Capital or three hundred volumes by the Marxists. That is the basic urge of freedom that created this world of men."[17]

Before his death in May 1905, Dinabandhu told his eldest son, Sushil, "Dona[18] has high ambitions; take care of him". Sushil and his sisters scrupulously respected their father's last wish.[19]

### NOTES AND REFERENCES

[1] A stalwart of Changripota revolutionaries, who died in Deoli Jail in 1937.

[2] Saileswar Bose started the shop "Universal Emporium" at Balasore in 1914.

[3] M. N. Roy, then Naren Bhattacharya, became Secretary of the Library

with Professor Charu Chandra Bhattacharya, later Secretary of the Visva-Bharati as the President (Interview with Alok Chakravarty).

4 Dr. Jadugopal: p. 117.

5 Harikumar: p. 3; Kalicharan Ghosh told me "Narenda used to climb coconut trees without any aid like squirrels".

6 Harikumar: p. 4.

7 Nalini Kar told me that when he first met M. N. Roy in the Anushilan Samity in 1906, Satish Bose introduced Roy to me saying "Naren has just come from Malda to here all the way—a distance of about 200 miles—on foot".

8 Interview with Lalit Bhattacharya.

9 One of Sivnarain Swami's disciples told a political leader: that of all his disciples Naren had become a true revolutionary and lived up to the Swami's expectation.

10 *Visva-Vivek*: p. 255.

11 Interview with Alok Chakravarty.

12 *Visva-Vivek*: p. 255.

13 Saileswar Bose opened the shop "Universal Emporium" at Balasore in 1914 which became the communication centre between Harikumar Chakravarty's "Harry and Sons" in Calcutta and Jatin Mukherjee's hiding resort at Mohandia, about 22 miles from Balasore at the time of planned armed uprising.

14 Harikumar: p. 6.

15 *Ibid.*: p. 6.

16 Prithwin Mukherjee's article in *Basumati* (Weely) dated 23rd September 1965.

17 M. N. Roy: *New Orientation*, p. 183.

18 Roy's nickname in the family.

19 Interview with Lalit Bhattacharya.

23

# III. Beginning of Revolutionary Politics

IN 1905, WHEN NAREN WAS A STUDENT AT A HIGH SCHOOL, Bengal was in a state of intense political ferment. The immediate cause was provided by the decision of the British Viceroy, Lord Curzon, to partition the province of Bengal on the ostensible ground of its being too unwieldy in geographic proportion. Bengal was determined to annul the partition. The revolutionary movement in Bengal was "worked on the top of what is known as the anti-partition agitation".[1] Young Bengal, under the impact of resurgent Hindu militancy, chose the path of 'direct action' against the elder statesmen's policy of meetings and petitions. Their idealism was provided by Bankim Chandra and Vivekananda. Teachings of Mazzini and Garibaldi inspired them. The Italian, French and Irish revolutions showed them the way. Success of Japan in the war against Russia in 1904 provided them with new hopes.

The decision of partition announced in July 1905, came into force from 16th October of the same year. The leaders of both parts of Bengal intensified the anti-partition agitation which engulfed a whole people and had begun at the time of Curzon's visit to Dacca in 1904 when the idea was mooted.

Thus, in 1905, for the first time in the history of Indian National Congress, its annual session opened with the *Bande Mataram*[2] song which subsequently became the national anthem of Indian patriots. Addressing the session, also for

24

the first time, Sister Nivedita, Vivekananda's ablest associate and a product of Irish nationalism, urged that attainment of political freedom should be the objective of the Indian people instead of individual spiritual *mukti* (salvation). And, in 1905, Aurobindo wrote and published the pamphlet, *Bhawani Mandir,* laying down the ideals and methods of revolution.

Naren came in touch with the Atmonnati Samity leaders like Indranath Nundy and others about this time, and began visiting anti-partition meetings in Calcutta. He always walked to Calcutta to attend these meetings and took with him some of his friends. His attendance of these meetings attracted the notice of the Headmaster of the School and he was given a warning to avoid such political associations.[3]

It was at such a time that Surendranath Banerjea, who had become famous as the "father of Indian Nationalism" was touring Bengal agitating against the British decision to truncate Bengal's Motherland. Naren arranged a public meeting for Surendranath in Kodalia. His visit to Kodalia provided Naren, then a high school student, with the urge to organise the meeting and a procession to welcome the honoured leader.[4]

Naren asked the new Headmaster of the school for permission to hold the meeting. When that was refused he decided to organise the procession and the meeting outside of school hours. But even then the wrath of the new government circular[5] fell on Naren and his seven friends, including Harikumar and Saileswar Bose, and they were rusticated from the school.[6]

Soon after, Naren told Harikumar: "The British cannot be driven out by meetings and petitions. They have to be driven out by force."[7]

At this crossroad of their lives they became "restless" to do something and to find out a path.[8] They received a copy of the revolutionary journal, *Sandhya,* founded and edited by Brahmabandhav Upadhyaya.[9] The editorial of the journal made a deep impression on them. It said: "We want complete independence. The country cannot prosper as long as the veriest shred of the Feringhee's supremacy over it is left. Swadeshi, boycott—all are meaningless to us, if they are not the means of retrieving our whole and complete independence."

About the same time, Kedarnath, uncle of Saileswar Bose, gave them Vivekananda's book, *Karma-Yoga.* Kedarnath was a member of Vivekananda Society and used to receive books from Sister Nivedita. Harikumar writes: "We read Vivekananda's message: 'It is better to be attached than to be unattached'. We were greatly excited. We had no sleep that night. Thereafter we read Swamiji's *Present India.* We then decided our course of life. Swamiji's philosophy of life provided us the guidelines; Vivekananda's words rang the bells in us. Henceforth food for thought and action came from his words. We began to sing his songs and chant his message: sacrifice."[10]

At this time, Ramdas Babaji sent for Naren and Harikumar again to pursuade them to seek spiritual path. "He talked with us the whole night. But his words fell on deaf ears. We had decided our course. Vivekananda's path was our path. Our god was our country. We had now before us the vision of Bankim Chandra's 'Mother that she would be'."[11]

Naren and Harikumar then met Swami Saradananda of Belur Math. Saradananda used to take classes on the Gita in the Anushilan Samity; and they were introduced to the Samity's Secretary, Satish Bose. They joined the Anushilan Samity towards the end of 1905,[12] and soon became close to Satish Bose.

In 1905 and 1906, Naren and Harikumar stayed at the central office of the Anushilan Samity at 49, Cornwallis Street[13] and commuted between that place and Changripota. They soon expanded their group and formed a branch of the Anushilan Samity at Changripota. A big show of physical culture, including wrestling and *lathi* play, was organised there in 1907 where Pulin Das of Dacca Anushilan Samity gave performances of *lathi* play.[14]

While staying at the central office of the Anushilan Samity, Naren studied the histories of revolutions, the lives of Mazzini, Garibaldi and other great men of history. He also took an active part in expanding the organisation of the Samity. When Nalini Kar, a close associate of Jatin Mukherjee, first met him in the Anushilan Samity in 1906, Naren had just returned from Malda where he was sent on an organisational mission.

The expulsion orders on Naren, Harikumar and his friends were subsequently withdrawn by the school authorities and they were asked to sit for their Entrance examination. But Naren and Harikumar took their fees from home and instead of depositing them for examination went to Orissa for famine relief work on behalf of the Anushilan Samity. Their performance in relief operations impressed the leaders of the Samity and on their return they were taken into the Inner Circle.[15] When admitted into the inner circle of the Samity, one had to hold a copy of the Gita with a sword placed above it and take the vow of liberating the country either in front of a sacrificial fire or the image of goddess Kali; and they had also to sign their names with their blood. When Naren and Harikumar were admitted into the inner circle, they refused to sign their names with blood. Naren told Satish Bose, "Is my word of honour not enough?".[16] Naren and Harikumar were admitted into the inner circle without having to sign their names with blood.

In Orissa, Naren was in charge of the Ruriahat camp at Jaipore which controlled relief operations in 12 centres. Dr. Aswini Roy, one of the earlier members of the Anushilan Samity, was later sent to Ruriahat by Satish Bose on receipt of a telegram that Harikumar had fallen ill. While there, Dr. Roy said: "One day I observed that Naren did not eat anything. That was the day of the full moon. After all the volunteers had finished their meal in the evening, I saw Naren walking up to the top of the dam wall. And then he sat there in the posture of *yogi* fixing his gaze on the moon. His eyelids never moved. He sat there in that posture until the moon went down. I watched him from a short distance all the time. When he came down I asked him why he had done this. He would not say anything. After repeated urgings, Naren said: 'Aswini, I am born in a poor family. There are so many great men in different parts of the world—I will never be able to meet them. So I look at the moon on the night of the full moon, hoping that if these men also looked at the bright moon from other parts of the world, there might be some communication with them through the moon'."[17]

Naren also showed keen interest in revolutionary journalism from the time he joined the Anushilan Samity. When staying at 49 Cornwallis Street, he used to regularly visit Kalinath Roy (later, Editor of *Tribune,* Lahore), then Subeditor of the *Bengalee* and Panchanan Majumdar of *New India* at the residence of Sasanka Joardar at Pataldanga.[18] It is not known whether Naren did any writing then, but sometime later, in 1907 or 1908, he wrote an article in *Jugantar,* captioned "Bharater Raja Ke?" (Who is India's Ruler?). In that article Naren wrote: "The voice of the people is the voice of god" and concluded that "it is only the people of India who can choose their own ruler. The British have imposed their rule over India and it is the birthright of the Indian people to defy and throw off the rule of the British from this country."[19] Naren used to study a lot at this time and he came to be considered one of the better read workers as well as one of the most intelligent and daring among them.[20]

An incident later raised Naren's position further in the estimation of Satish Bose. This was at the time of the *Ardhodaya Yoga* in February 1908. At the time of *Ardhodaya Yoga,* a large number of pilgrims, mostly women, congregated in Calcutta from far and near for the holy dip in the river Ganges. The Anushilan Samity had provided volunteers for rendering help to the pilgrims. A report reached the office of the Samity that some British Highlanders were behaving improperly with women pilgrims by moving them by means of their batons to keep clear the flow of people. Satish Bose was upset. Dr. Aswini Roy suggested firing on the Highlanders from a distance. Naren intervened and said that firing would lead to serious consequences; besides there would be counteraction by both police and military followed by governmental repressive measure against members of the Samity on suspicion.

Instead, Naren asked for four strong volunteers and told them to carry with them short wooden rods hidden under their sleeves. With these four volunteers (they were: Aswini Roy, Bholanath Chatterjee, Dr. Rasik Lal Dutt and Nagen Dutt), Naren went to the Esplanade area. He first checked whether the report about the Highlanders was correct and then asked his friends to take positions behind the Highlanders. He told them to wait for his signal and then hit the Highlanders on the ear just below their caps and immediately board the running trams keeping their rods with them to protect themselves against possible trouble inside the tram.

After they returned successfully carrying out Naren's instructions, other Anushilan members, who were keeping watch, reported that all five of the Highlanders fell on the ground unconscious and had to be removed to the Hospital. The Highlanders were immediately withdrawn from the area without any repercussion.

Satish Bose was so pleased with this operation that he remarked: "Naren, one day you will be somebody in our ranks."[21]

## NOTES AND REFERENCES

[1] Sir Charles Tegart: *Terrorism in India* (Speech before the Royal Empire Society on 1st November 1932), p. 7.

[2] B. B. Majumdar: p. 51.

[3] Interview with Alok Chakravarty.

[4] Surendranath Banerjea was accompanied by Bipin Chandra Pal, Mokshada Samadhyayee and Indranath Nundy in this trip. Mokshada Samadhyayee was associated with the journal, *Sandhya,* and Indranath Nundy belonged to the Atmonnati Samity at the time (as told by Alok Chakravarty). See also Harikumar, pp. 5-6.

[5] An Anti-Circular Society was formed at this time to agitate against the government circular prohibiting students from participating in anti-partition meetings and processions. (See also Amales Tripathi: *The Extremist Challenge,* pp. 119-21.)

[6] Harikumar: p. 6.

[7] Interview with Kalicharan Ghosh.

[8] Harikumar: p. 7.

[9] *Ibid.*: p. 7.

[10] *Visva-Vivek*: p. 254.

Lord Ronaldshay, then Governor of Bengal, visited Harikumar Chakravarty in the Dacca Jail in 1916 and asked him: "Are you a follower of Vivekananda?". Harikumar replied: "certainly so". "Perhaps", Harikumar wrote "he wanted to ascertain whose influence was behind the revolutionary movement. There was no revolutionary in those days who did not have a book of Vivekananda at his home" (*Visva-Vivek*: p. 253).

[11] *Visva-Vivek*: p. 254.

[12] M. N. Roy: *Life and Thought* (Bengali Pamphlet), published by Mukundalal Sarkar, 1958, p. 4; also interview with Dr. Jadugopal Mukherjee, Hem Chandra Ghosh, Sarat Chandra Ghosh. Dr. Jadugopal wrote in Dr. Bhupen Dutta's book, "I met Naren Bhattacharya first in the Anushilan Samity in 1905 along with Harikumar Chakravarty." [Dr. Bhupen Dutt, *Aprakasita Rajnaitik Itihas* (Unpublished Political History of India), Nava-Bharat Publishers, Calcutta, 1953, p. 197.]

[13] Interview with Kali Charan Ghosh.

[14] *Ibid.*

[15] Interview with Sarat Chandra Ghosh.

[16] Interview with Kali Charan Ghosh.

[17] As told by Dr. Aswini Roy.

[18] Interview with Sarat Chandra Ghosh. Ghosh believed that Naren used to write for the journals.

[19] As told by Nirvan Swami who quoted the text from memory. It was not possible for me to secure any copy of the journal, *Jugantar*, although a few persons confirmed that such an article had appeared in *Jugantar*.

[20] Interview with Hem Chandra Ghosh and Haridas Dutt.

[21] Interview with Dr. Aswini Roy.

# IV. Jatin Mukherjee

SOON AFTER THE FOUNDING OF THE CIRCULAR ROAD CENTRE, tension developed between Jatindranath Banerjee and Barin Ghosh; and as a result Jatindranath left the Circular Road residence in 1903 and moved to a boarding house in Sitaram Ghosh Street. From there he carried on his political activity in collaboration with Jogendra Nath Vidyabhusan. Jogendra Vidyabhusan had rendered into Bengali the lives of Garibaldi and Mazzini which had become popular with the revolutionaries and were text-books in the Anushilan Samity's political classes. At the request of both Jatindranath (Banerjee), whom he regarded highly as his political associate[1] and his brother, Barin, Aurobindo came to Calcutta to resolve the dispute and stayed at the house of Jogendra Vidyabhusan.

During Aurobindo's stay at Calcutta, Jatin Mukherjee[2] was introduced to Aurobindo by Vidyabhusan's son, Sachindranath, whom Jatin Mukherjee had come to know at the *Akhara* (gymnasium) of Ambar Guha. When Jatin Mukherjee met him, Aurobindo spoke to him about his three-pronged plan:

(1) (a) "To initiate the youth to the idea of developing physical and military strength.

(b) To build up secret societies and preach revolutionary idea.

(c) Make preparations for armed revolution.

31

(2) To make Indians realise the value of freedom and make them conscious about freedom by launching campaigns through journals, newspapers and public speeches.

(3) To develop public organisation to fight through non-cooperation, passive resistance, boycott of foreign goods and the building up of "a state within state".

Aurobindo also urged: Boycott of foreign-dominated educational institutions, organisation of national educational institutions; starting of people's courts and promulgation of new laws; organisation of volunteer corps and their gradual transformation into a National Army.

The liberal nationalist leaders aimed at the achievement of Dominion Status under the British. The militant nationalist leaders led by Aurobindo went a step further and aimed at complete independence from British rule.

As the chief theoretician and the propounder of this new school of thought, Aurobindo advocated violent means but did not rule out non-violent methods for preparing the masses. In fact, the concept of passive resistance—non-violent Satyagraha—was first advocated by Aurobindo through his journal, *Bande Mataram*. But Aurobindo and Bipin Pal conceived of passive resistance not as a means for independence but, to a greater extent, to widen popular response and participation in the struggle for independence.

While talking to Jatin Mukherjee, Aurobindo had argued that many outside powers and nations would be interested in helping India achieve her freedom. After this meeting, Jatin Mukherjee became a close follower of Aurobindo and actively engaged himself in the collection of arms, money and men.[3]

Soon thereafter Jatin Mukherjee organised the "Chatra Bhandar" with Nikhileswar Roy Moulik, Kartick Dutt, Indranath Nandy, Pavitra Dutt and others. The volunteers were mainly supplied by Satish Bose from the different branches of the Anushilan Samity. The "Chatra Bhandar" was started as a "Students' Cooperative Store Association". This became an important coordination centre for revolutionaries and having access to the confidential files of the government as a stenographer Jatin Mukherjee used to fore-warn the revolutionaries about government actions through the *Chatra Bhandar.*

Sometime in the later part of 1906, Naren first met Jatin Mukherjee and eventually became an ardent follower of the latter.

Naren was closely associated with Barin Ghosh when the latter started his bomb-making centre at Muraripukur Gardens in Manicktolla. Barin at this time formed a group of his own with Aurobindo as the leader.[4] Jatin Mukherjee was also associated with the group and so was Naren. Soon after, two incidents happened. Barin developed an antipathy to Jatin Mukherjee and one day remarked about Jatin Mukherjee: "How can a government servant be a revolu-tionary?"[5] The comment reached Jatin Mukherjee's ears. He was disappointed and stopped visiting Manicktolla gar-dens thereafter.

Barin at this time could not stand his followers visiting other leaders, in particular Jatin Mukherjee, who was be-coming very popular with younger men by his affectionate nature and non-group attitude as well as for his heroic kill-ing of a tiger without arms. This later had earned him the title "Bagha" (Tiger) Jatin.

About this time by the end of 1907, Naren's cousin, Phani Chakravarty returned to Calcutta from Darjeeling where he had met and become intimate with Jatin Mukherjee. Jatin Mukherjee had asked Phani to get in touch with Naren and others of Changripota[6] and inspired him (Phani) into nationalist politics. On his return Phani became friend-ly with Naren and through Naren with Barin. But Phani went on visiting Jatin Mukherjee which displeased Barin. One day Barin asked Phani not to see Jatin Mukherjee. Meanwhile Barin's remark about Jatin Mukherjee had caused some bitterness among other followers too and did not please Aurobindo who was fond of Jatin Mukherjee. After Phani was rebuked by Barin for his meeting Jatin Mukherjee, Naren grew more curious to know Jatin Mukherjee, and met him privately along with Phani. After

33

C

the meeting, Naren also snapped his relationship with Barin and became close to Jatin Mukherjee.

Naren describes this incident in a dramatic manner in his own words: "I overheard a few sentences of a conversation. I still belonged to the entourage of another 'dada' (dada literally means elder brother but in this context means leader of a group), and heard him rebuking a 'chela' (follower) presumably for wavering loyalty. The latter had been visiting some other *dada*. Ultimately, in exasperation, the suspected apostate rejoined mildly: 'Dada, why do you want me not to see him, when he does not want me to join his party; he has no party'. I was curious to know who was that strange sort of a *dada*, and buttonholed the rebuked *gurubhai* (fellow disciple) after he was dismissed by the extremely annoyed *dada*. The next day I was taken to the unusual *dada* who did not play the game of 'chela-dhara' (netting disciples) and was caught for good. At that time I did not know what was the attraction...later on, I realised what attracted me: it was his personality. Since then I have had the privilege of meeting outstanding personalities of our time. These are great men. Jatinda was a good man and I still have to find a better. All *Dadas* practised magnetism; only Jatin Mukherjee possessed it."[7]

Jatin Mukherjee advised Naren, Harikumar and Phani Chakravarty to develop social service activity and carry on revolutionary preparations in secret under the cover of social service.[8] Soon after their meeting with Jatin Mukherjee, Naren and Harikumar went to Chhedapahar hill in Bankura on the south-west border of Bengal to learn bomb-making and practice shooting. They soon organised a group of about 40/45 revolutionaries who believed in 'direct action'. In the group were Dr. Sarat Mitter of Kidderpore, Charu Ghosh of Chetla and Hem Sen of Netra. A Muslim inhabitant of Chetla, Nur Mohammad, who was an expert in gun repairing and was himself a dealer in arms, sold to this group a fairly large number of guns which were kept in the house of Charu Ghosh. The group later started shooting practice in the Sunderbans.[9]

## NOTES AND REFERENCES

1 Jatindranath Banerjee claimed that it was he who influenced Aurobindo while in Baroda to participate actively in revolutionary politics. (Interview with Dr. Jadugopal Mukherjee.)

2 Jatin Mukherjee first met Swami Vivekananda at a reception at the Sovabazar Rajbati and was profoundly impressed by his speech. Later, during the plague epidemic in Calcutta he came to know Vivekananda more closely while working for the relief operations. Nivedita wrote about Jatin Mukherjee that "a young man came to see me whose one idea was to make Swamiji's name the rallying point for young India". (Prithwin Mukherjee's article in *Basumati,* dated 23rd September 1965.)

3 Prithwin Mukherjee's article in *Basumati,* 23rd September 1965.

4 Interview with Dr. Jadugopal Mukherjee.

5 Interview with Dr. Jadugopal Mukherjee.

6 Interview with Alok Chakravarty.

7 M. N. Roy: "Jatin Mukherjee" (article in *Independent India,* 27th February 1949).

8 Interview with Alok Chakravarty.

9 Interview with Alok Chakravarty.

# V. Political Murder and Dacoities

BY THE MIDDLE OF 1906, BARIN WAS "FED UP" WITH THE LATHI play organisation of Anushilan Samity and decided that the country should be stirred up in the revolutionary way by revolutionary propaganda and actions. Barin and his friends decided to publish the journal, *Jugantar,* to preach revolution. This led to the conflict between Barin and Pramatha Mitra. Soon afterwards in March 1906, Barin, Avinash Bhattacharya and Bhupen Dutt (younger brother of Swami Vivekananda) started the Journal, *Jugantar.* To resolve the growing conflict between Barin's group, and Pramatha Mitra, an All-Bengal Revolutionary Conference was held at the house of Subodh Mullick about this time. Pramatha agreed at the conference to support Barin's journal; nevertheless, the conflict between the two groups went on increasing. Pramatha Mitra believed that unless proper organisational network was formed it would be premature to think of rebellion. Any premature action, Pramatha Mitra believed, would lead to disruption of whatever organisational basis has been formed.

Soon thereafter, Jatindranath Banerjee left Calcutta because of continued tension with Barin. Jatindranath Banerjee travelled at this time through U. P. and Punjab and inspired Sardar Aijt Singh and others into revolutionary politics. At this time, Jatindranath Banerjee became a *sanyasi* and adopted the *Sanyas* name, Niralamba Swami.

Jatin Mukherjee also lost his eldest son about this time

and went to Hardwar to become a *sanyasi*. In Hardwar, Jatin Mukherjee met Bholananda Giri, his religious *guru,* who inspired him afresh in politics. Bholananda Giri was a well-known *sadhu* in whose *ashram* many revolutionaries took shelter and later became his disciple. Bholananda Giri told him: "You have yet to contribute a lot to the country's cause." In this trip, Jatin Mukherjee also met Niralamba Swami and became his political disciple. Jatin Mukherjee later took the advice of Niralamba Swami in all the major political decisions that he took. Returning to Calcutta, Jatin Mukherjee actively engaged himself in revolutionary activity. He not only associated himself with the bomb-making centre of Barin Ghosh at Manicktolla but began to organise different groups in pursuance of the plan to eventually wage war against the British.

Meanwhile, Naren had also come close to Barin with whom he had earlier came in contact through his Arbelia cousin, Avinash Bhattacharya. Naren did not dissociate himself with the Anushilan Samity but he was staying with Barin and Avinash at the boarding house at Bhawani Dutt Lane in 1907.[1] While staying at the Chatra Bhandar Mess at Bhawani Dutt Lane, Naren at the request of Barin Ghosh, wrote a booklet in Bengali titled, *Mayer Dak* (The Mother's Call). The manuscript of the book was seized by the police from his person when he was arrested in connection with the Changripota Railway Station Dacoity[2] and it never saw the light of the day. Naren had by then learned the technique of making bombs. About this time Naren also began to express himself against *lathi* play as a means for political revolution, in opposition to Pramatha Mitra and Satish Bose of Anushilan Samity. He told Dr. Aswini Roy about this time: "These are not the right ways. There must be some other way for the achievement of freedom. We have to find that way."[3] Naren evinced greater interest in politics and methods of revolution at this time and was groping for an effective means. It was at this time that Naren showed greater interest in the three-pronged plan of Aurobindo that the latter had spoken about to Jatin Mukherjee. This had brought Naren closer to Jatin

Mukherjee than other leaders at that time, and thus when Naren met him along with Phani Chakravarty, the talk led to their firm association in the future.

In the latter part of 1907 a series of terrorist activities were inspired by the revolutionaries in which the journals, *Sandhya, Jugantar* and *Bande Mataram* provided inspiration. (An account of the literature and press of the revolutionaries is given in the appendix.) There were various opinions among the revolutionaries in regard to murder and dacoity. While most revolutionaries approved of terrorising the administration, Jatin Mukherjee was opposed to murders unless absolutely necessary for self-protection, and rejected dacoity as a means of raising funds. Only twice did Jatin Mukherjee agree to dacoity, once in 1908-9, and again in 1914 after he was elected supreme commander following the declaration of the first world war. Naren, according to Satish Chakravarty, was unconcerned about the moral question involved in murder and violence. Satish Chakravarty added: to Naren political murder and dacoity came easily and did not trouble his conscience at all. Some others, like Dr. Jadugopal Mukherjee, approved murder and dacoity if Britishers and British money were involved. Thus, there was no uniform opinion and in fact, there was no uniform, planned manner in which murder and dacoity were committed by the revolutionaries.

Two unsuccessful attempts were made near Chandernagore and Mankundu—both on the Eastern Railway in the Hooghly District—to blow up the Governor's train in October 1907. On 6th December, the revolutionaries were partly successful in derailing the Governor's train at Narayangarh near Midnapur by a bomb. The revolutionaries had been procuring firearms from Chandernagore—then a French enclave in British India—for their terroristic activities. This was stopped by an Ordinance of the Mayor of Chandernagore. A bomb was thrown at the Mayor's residence in retaliation on 11th April 1908.

The revolutionaries at this time needed funds for making bombs and procuring firearms. A series of dacoities was therefore planned. The first of these dacoities was committed by Naren at the Changripota Railway Station on 6th December 1907. When he was arrested, a copy of Barin Ghosh's *Bartaman Rananiti* (Strategy of Modern Warfare) and the manuscript titled *Mayer Dak* (The Mother's Call) were found in his possession.[4] Naren was released on bail, his reputation as a social worker in the area having helped him.[5] The case was not pursued. In the application for bail before the Police Magistrate of Sealdah in Calcutta, the lawyer, Babu Promotho Nath Mukherjee, stated that "the youth was a student of the Bengal Technical Institute and passed the Entrance Examination (School Leaving examination) of the National College and got a medal".[6]

After the Changripota dacoity, Naren absconded and was arrested at the station while returning to Changripota. But since his enlargement on bail, Naren had been mostly in hiding and returned to Changripota shortly before his mother died on the morning of 5th *Magh* 1315 B.S. (January 1908) and stayed until his mother's *sradh* was performed. In keeping with the Hindu tradition, Naren shaved his head, his elder brother Sushil performing the *Yajna*.

For three or four days before her death, Naren's widowed mother in delirium wanted to eat stew of meat. Naren requested Dr. Aswini Roy who was also acting as a visiting physician, to give her meat stew when she wanted it so much. But because of opposition of his elder brother Sushil and his wife—eating fish, meat, etc. is prohibited for the Hindu widow—she could not be given meat. Naren was hurt but had no option because of the family's opposition on grounds of tradition and orthodoxy.

About this time Naren and Harikumar committed a large number of dacoities in Eastern Bengal and Naren became an expert in river dacoity. Recalling one of those dacoities (as narrated to him by Harikumar) Kali Charan Ghosh told me that one day before leaving a house, after committing dacoity, Naren was snatching a gold chain from the neck of a small girl, when Harikumar caught him (Naren) by the neck. Naren almost fainted and had to promise to Harikumar that never again would he do such things.[7]

After starting the *Jugantar* newspaper Barin was soon fed up and thought this was not enough. He decided to give the charge of the journal to others and set up the bomb manufacturing centre at Manicktolla gardens in 1907. He now wanted some terrorist actions so as to further stir up the revolutionary fervour.

The bomb throwing soon thereafter, under Aurobindo's inspiration, at the carriage in which Mrs. and Miss Kennedys were returning from the club in Muzaffarpur, mistaking them for the 'notorious' Kingsford, led the police to the discovery of the Manicktolla conspiracy and led to the Alipore Bomb Case, in which Aurobindo and Barin Ghosh, Ullaskar Dutt, Avinash Bhattacharya, Hem Chandra Das (Kanungo), Upendranath Banerjee and others were arrested and all, except Aurobindo, convicted to various terms of imprisonment.

However, when police came to arrest them at the Manicktolla gardens, Barin told his revolutionary colleagues: "My mission is over",[8] which dispirited the group. In fact, Barin's group was thoroughly disrupted thereafter. While in jail during trial, Aurobindo began to take greater interest in spiritual development and intensely practised *yoga*. Aurobindo, the principal accused, was acquitted by the judge partly because of the intense emotional appeal of his Counsel, C. R. Das, and also because the whole court and the judge were moved by his spiritual transformation.

During the trial several murders had also taken place. Naren Gossain the principal approver, was shot dead in August 1908 inside the jail by Kanai Dutt. "Had he not murdered Naren Gossain, it would have been difficult to save Aurobindo from long term of imprisonment."[9] In November of the same year, Nandalal Banerjee, a sub-Inspector in the Intelligence Branch was shot dead in Calcutta for his part in the arrest of Prafulla Chaki, the associate of Khudiram Bose in the Muzaffarpur assassination attempt. After the murder of Nandalal Banerjee, a day and night police camp was set up near the house of absconding Naren at Changripota. In a letter written lately by Bhupendra Kumar Dutt to Naren's nephew, Alok Chakravarty, on 16th

June 1963, Dutt writes: "Naren Bhattacharya, Bhusan Mitra and Naren Bose of Atmonnati Samity shot Nandalal Banerjee the I. B. agent, who was sent to arrest Khudiram. This was organised by Hem Sen of Netra (near Diamond Harbour, in District 24 Parganas), who was a favourite of Jatin Mukherjee."[10] On 10th February 1910, the Deputy Superintendent of Police in charge of the prosecution case, Shamsul Alam, was also shot dead inside the court premises by Birendranath Dutt Gupta.

On his acquittal, Aurobindo felt rather lonely and openly condemned violence. On 17th July 1909, at a meeting at College Square, he urged people to "suffer" instead of retaliating when repression came. About this time Sister Nivedita warned Aurobindo that the government was thinking of deporting him to Burma. Thus, on the day Shamsul Alam was murdered, he decided to leave Calcutta forthwith and left for Chandernagore the same day and after a brief stay of about two months, went to Pondicherry.[11] Aurobindo lived there as a religious recluse till his death in 1951 abjuring active politics.

The arrest of Aurobindo and Barin and their group, the subsequent desertion of Aurobindo from active politics and the long-term imprisonment of Barin and others threw the terrorist-revolutionaries into wilderness, disillusionment and confusion. The Anushilan Samity had also been banned at that time. Naren "could not accept the closure of the Anushilan Samity and began meeting Jatin Mukherjee frequently to give the government a fitting reply".[12]

It was from this time that Naren and Jatin Mukherjee drew close to each other. In order to pursue organisational work and revolutionary activities, two centres were established in 1908. One was the 'Sramajibi Samabaya' headed by Amarendra Nath Chattopadhyaya of Uttarpara which opened its office on Harrison Road, close to the Presidency College. Amarendra Nath Chattopadhyaya was a class-mate of Upen Banerjee, an accused in the Alipore Bomb Case and a close associate of Barin Ghosh, and entered politics as a sympathiser of the Jugantar group of Barin Ghosh. He joined Jatin Mukherjee actively in 1908. The other centre was opened at Raja Woodmunt Street in the heart of the commercial area in Dalhousie Square in the name of "S. D. Harry and Sons" from where Harikumar Chakravarty began to operate. Both were ostensible places of business.[13] Naren and Jatin Mukherjee began to coordinate their activities mainly through these two centres. With his bold and defiant attitude and affectionate nature, Jatin Mukherjee endeared himself to the revolutionaries greatly. Those who helped him build up revolutionary activity from this time included Naren Bhattacharya, Atul Krishna Ghosh, Amarendra Nath Chattopadhyaya, Harikumar Chakravarty and a few others, and the movement since then was guided by this collective leadership.

Dr. Aswini Roy told me in his interview: "After the Anushilan Samity was banned, a large number of people left revolutionary politics, including myself. Most of us were not politicians only, to us it was an urge which we satisfied by participating in the cause of the Motherland keeping our other professions undisturbed. Naren was different. Politics, freedom of the country were the sole missions of his life." It was from this time that Naren rose in the leadership hierarchy. With his untiring energy, he contacted different leaders and groups to forge some kind of coordinated group. In fact, Naren initiated a new beginning. Aurobindo had left politics; Barin's group was broken up and the Anushilan Samity was banned; Naren began with what was left over.

Several dacoities were committed by Naren and Jatin Mukherjee at this time to raise funds for political activities. One of the dacoities that Naren committed was at Netra, near Diamond Harbour in 24 Parganas District on 25th April 1909. When leaving with the loot, Naren in mask, told the owner of the house: "We are only borrowing the money to drive the British away."[14] The dacoity yielded about Rs. 2,000.

Naren was arrested in connection with this dacoity but was released on bail on 1st June 1909. After obtaining bail, he absconded and mostly stayed at Shibpur in Howrah. After that the two Muktears who stood bail for Naren in the Netra Case were paid their forfeited surety money from the funds of the revolutionaries.

While in Howrah, Naren carried on political discussions with various groups and was planning guerilla type warfare and other means to drive the British out of this country. Interviewed by the author, Nirvan Swami, who met Naren frequently those days and was later put in charge of conducting the defence case in the Howrah Conspiracy Case as an absconding accused said: "Naren's political thinking was much ahead of others and he was intensely a political revolutionary." "Naren", according to Nirvan Swami, "held socialistic views and never mixed religion with politics".[15] Naren used to talk about what kind of government he wanted in replacement of the British Government and he thought of a "People's Government" as distinct from the government of a privileged few, and he thought the only way that such a government could be formed was through the revolutionary means of attainment of freedom. Bhupati Mazumdar also averred that Naren was 'our leader' those days and discussed politics "in a much more advanced way than most of us".

Bhupati Mazumdar said that it was Naren's idea in those day's in regard to rural economy to eliminate the *Jotedars* (big holders of cultivable lands) first because it was they who exploited the smaller and the landless peasantry more than the big landlords.[16]

### NOTES AND REFERENCES

[1] Interview with Purna Sen.

[2] *Vide;* "Prosecution Charge against Naren Bhattacharya in Howrah Gang Case", *CWN,* Vol. XV.

[3] Interview with Dr. Aswini Roy.

[4] *CWN.,* Vol. XV, p. 614.

[5] Kali Charan Ghosh (born 1890), author of *The Roll of Honour* told me in an interview that people of Kodalia, Changripota and the adjacent villages used to salute the dust of the path "Narenda" and "Harida" travelled and narrated the following as one of the many social services that they used to render. The entire family of eight of one Ambika Mitra of Sankaripara, Changripota, was once laid down with Cholera. The family was poor, and there was nobody to render any

assistance. Narenda, Harida and Saileswar went to the house, did all the cleaning and nursing of the family day and night for several days without rest; and even cooked food for them. Narenda used to carry the bile excretions of the patients in his own hands and dump them in the ground outside the hut. Harida administered homeopathic medicine. We were young and we used to wait outside if we should ever be called for any work either for messenger service or anything else. Five out of eight patients survived. Kali Charan Ghosh, who also hails from Changripota, said: similar tales of social service of the group and of personal "heroism" of Narenda were unlimited. Narenda was available for any kind of social service. He added: "When I asked Harikumar in later days why did they do so. Harikumar smilingly replied, 'Why else would people follow us?' ".

6 *Amrita Bazar Patrika,* 11th December 1907.

7 Interview with Kalicharan Ghosh.

8 Interview with Purna Sen.

9 Biman Behari Mazumdar : *Militant Nationalism in India,* p. 112.

10 Confirmed to me by Bhupendra Kumar Dutt during my interview with him.

11 Interview with Nirvan Swami.

12 Dr. Jadugopal: p. 341.

13 Dr. Jadugopal: p. 421.

14 *Ibid.:* p. 340; also Prithwin Mukherjee's serialised biography of Jatin Mukherjee in *Basumati* (Weekly), p. 1494.

15 Interview with Nirvan Swami. Dr. Jadugopal Mukherjee also said the same things in his interview with me. In his *Memoirs,* M. N. Roy writes: "We all shared the same vague desire to uplift the poor and the down-trodden. Bankim Chandra's *Ananda Math* was our common source of inspiration" (*Memoirs,* p. 98).

16 Interview with Bhupati Majumdar.

# VI. Howrah Conspiracy Case

AFTER THE MURDER OF SHAMSUL ALAM, BIREN DUTTA GUPTA was arrested and tried in the court of the Presidency Magistrate, Calcutta. This led to the arrest of the persons accused in the Howrah Conspiracy Case which was being prepared by Shamsul Alam before his death.

Biren, however, refused to say anything in the Presidency Magistrate's Court and was committed to Sessions in the High Court. At this point, an Intelligence Officer had a forged copy of the journal of the revolutionaries, *Jugantar,* printed, carrying slanders against Biren in order to provoke him. When shown that copy, Biren said: "Let others spread canard against me as much as they can, I am proud to have the support of one man." Asked, who that man was, Biren named Jatin Mukherjee.[1]

After being sentenced to death, Biren was brought to the Howrah Jail where Jatin Mukherjee was also detained under arrest on the murder charge. Biren identified Jatin Mukherjee there. But Jatin's lawyer expressed inability to cross-examine Biren that day. Next day, Biren was hanged. As Biren was not cross-examined, this technical lapse on the part of the Prosecution saved Jatin Mukherjee from being hanged on the same charge. But in the meantime, all the other accused in the Howrah Conspiracy Case were arrested. Because of Government inability to establish their case through proper and reliable evidence, they were all acquitted in April 1911. Thus, Shamsul Alam's murder was at least partly vindicated.

It is in the Howrah Conspiracy Case that government classified the accused into different groups and named Jugantar as one of the groups[2] involved in the conspiracy to overthrow the British Government by force.

Naren was arrested from the house of one 'Bajrang' in Shibpur[3] and kept in solitary confinement for more than six months. During the period of his solitary confinement, Naren practised *yoga* which he had learned from Sivnarain Swami as well as *Raj yoga* of Vivekananda.[4] Altogether 44 accused persons[5] including Naren and Jatin Mukherjee were arrested in the case, most of them being taken into custody on 29th January 1910. The magisterial enquiry commenced on 4th March 1910 and the accused persons were committed to trial before a Special Tribunal of the High Court on 20th July 1910.

The committal order charged the accused persons that "between the Christian years of 1905 and 1910, both inclusive, at Shibpur, in the District of Howrah and at other places in British India, did conspire with one another and with other persons, to wit the following: Lalit Chakravarty, Jatindranath Hazra, Satish Chandra Sarkar,[6] Birendranath Dutta Gupta,[7] Barindra Kumar Ghosh,[8] Hem Chandra Das,[9] Ullaskar Dutt,[10] Avinash Chandra Bhattacharya,[11] Shishir Kumar Ghosh and other persons unknown, to wage war against His Majesty the King Emperor and deprive the King Emperor of the sovereignty of British India and to overawe by means of criminal force the Government of India by law established and thereby committed an offence punishable under Section 121A of the Indian Penal Code".[12]

Jatindranath Hazra and Lalit Kumar Chakravarty became approvers in the case.

The Howrah Gang Case, as it came to be commonly called, mentioned a series of political dacoities committed in different part of Bengal and revealed, for the first time, the group's alleged complicity in tampering with the loyalty of the sepoys of the 10th Jat Regiment[13] which was later disbanded as a result.

The Prosecution sought to connect the conspiracy with "a large number of crimes of a political nature which included murder of two police officers and of an informer, collection of arms and ammunitions, and attempt to tamper with the loyalty of some sepoys of the 10th Jat Regiment and a large number of dacoities carried out by '*bhadralogs*' with the object of securing funds for the purpose of the conspiracy". The *Jugantar* newspaper and the Chatra Bhandar were also sought to be connected with the conspiracy.[14] Following the setting up of the Manicktolla centre in 1907, Barin's group handed over the charge of the Jugantar newspaper to Jatin Mukherjee's group. For a long time the paper was in charge of Kiron Mukherjee who was deputed by Jatin Mukherjee to look after the newspaper. It was at this time that Naren also took interest in the journal and occasionally wrote articles.

It was during detention under trial in this case that they formed the nucleus of what may be called the most militant group of nationalist revolutionaries and planned to launch a guerilla war against the government. The group timed this guerilla war to be launched around 1920 basing their calculation on the possibility of a world war around that time, and availability of help from foreign powers, particularly, Germany and Turkey, for their war against the British Government in India.[15] They received their informations about the possibility of war between England and Germany not only through the men of the 10th Jat Regiment with whom the revolutionaries had maintained good connections but also through their own emissaries sent abroad.

The Manicktolla conspirators did not concern themselves with anything beyond manufacture of bombs for the purpose of terrorising British administrators. The idea was primarily mooted by Barin Ghosh. Barin's idea had led to sharp differences between him and Jatindranath Banerjee. The latter also believed in violence but for the bigger object of overthrowing the British rule by an armed uprising which needed extensive organisation.

Barin's idea was "to stir up the revolutionary fervour" of the Bengalis and to manufacture bombs for that limited purpose. That is why when the police arrived at the

Muraripukur Garden to arrest Barin and his group, Barin said that his "mission is over". The whole Manicktolla conspiracy was in fact exposed following the abortive attempt to bomb the carriage of Kingsford, who, as Presidency Magistrate in Calcutta, had incurred much unpopularity by awarding heavy punishment to students accused of seditious activity. According to Dr. Jadugopal Mukherjee, a bench of revolutionaries consisting of Aurobindo Ghosh, Charu Dutta and Subodh Mullick had earlier sentenced Kingsford to death, and deputed Khudiram, then a young boy of 19 and a recruit of Satyen Bose of Midnapur, and Prafulla Chaki, another young boy of tender age, to put an end to the life of Kingsford.[16]

The idea of terrorism came from Barin Ghosh who held the belief that it was possible to provoke the worst of coward to commit murder and sacrifice his own self for the sake of the Motherland if properly fed upon the idea.[17]

The Howrah conspirators, in sharp distinction from their Manicktolla compatriots, were not content with mere terroristic activity and held much deeper political motives and aspirations. The Howrah Gang Case revealed that the groups were actively planning an insurrection against the government through, first, building a nucleus of organisational network throughout Bengal, maintaining links with other parts of the country; second, raising funds for political purposes by committing dacoities; third, by establishing links with the sepoys in the British Indian army and fourth, through procuring firearms.

The first phase of the militant nationalist movement ended with the Howrah Gang Case. The Manicktolla Conspiracy Case had disrupted and thrown into disarray the group that had centred round Barin and Aurobindo Ghoshes. Jatindranath Banerjee left for Brindaban following his release from the Alipore Bomb Case for want of evidence. On his acquittal, Aurobindo later left for Pondicherry giving up active politics. The fates of Barin and others were sealed with long terms of imprisonment. The ban on the Anushilan Samity and the Atmonnati Samity in Calcutta had come on 11th December 1908 and had disrupted the organisations of these groups. The arrest later, of Pulin Das, Anushilan's most efficient organiser in Dacca, caused the death of Pramatha Mitra, Anushilan Samity's agile President, from the shock. What remained of Anushilan Samity thereafter was confined mostly to Dacca and the party came to be known as the Anushilan Samity of Dacca. In January 1909, however, the Dacca Anushilan Samity along with Swadesh Bandhab Samity of Bakerganj, the Brati Samity of Faridpur, the Suhrid and Sadhana Samities of Mymensingh were also declared unlawful organisations.

At this point, it fell upon Jatin Mukherjee and Naren to bring the groups together which eventually came to be known as the Jugantar Party. The political manoeuvres and organisational planning of this federated group was done by Naren Bhattacharya with the active support of Jatin Mukherjee. And this brought the two even closer. In fact, Naren's organisational ability and the contribution of the Changripota group towards the building up of what eventually came to be known as the Jugantar Party was so much that Jatin Mukherjee chose him as his second in command.

#### NOTES AND REFERENCES

[1] Dr. Jadugopal: p. 339.

[2] The names of other groups as recorded were Krishnagar group, Haludbari group, Rajshahi group, Shibpur group, Kidderpore group, Majilpur group and the Chhatra Bhandar group, Dr. Jadugopal: pp. 44-45.

[3] Nirvan Swami who gave me the information could not recollect the full name of Bajrang.

[4] Swadesh Ranjan Das: *Manabendranath*, p. 43.

[5] The 44 accused persons were: Nanigopal Sen Gupta, Bhudan Mukherjee, Bhutan Mukherjee, Bistupada Chatterjee, Jogesh Chandra Mitter, Atul Mukherjee, Ganesh Das, Narendranath Bose, Harendranath Banerjee, Soilendra Kumar Das, Rajani Bhattacharya, Indu Kiron Bhattacharya (alias Chakravarty), Tincori Das, Chunilal Nandy, Bidhu Bhusan Biswas, Sushil Kumar Biswas, Monmotho Nath Biswas, Bijoy Chakravarty, Srish Chandra Sarkar, Narendranath Bhattacharya (M. N. Roy), Bhusan Chandra Mitter, Bimola Charan Deb, Sarat Chandra Mitter (Dr.), Suresh Chandra Mitter, Upendra Nath De, Kalipada Chakravarty, Soilendra Nath Chatterjee, Dasarathi Chatterjee, Shibu Hazra, Atul Pal, Monmotho Nath Rai Chaudhury, Kiron Chandra Rai, Nibaran Chandra Mazumdar, Suresh

D

Chandra Mazumdar (founder of *Ananda Bazar Patrika*), Jatindra Nath Mukherjee, Charu Chandra Ghosh, Pulin Behari Sarkar (alias Mitra), Ramapada Mukherjee, Bhupendra Nath Rai Chaudhury, Taranath Rai Chaudhuri, Kartick Chandra Dutt, Pabitra Dutt, Ananda Rai and Narendra Nath Chatterjee.

6 Satish Chandra Sarkar is the former name of Nirvan Swami who was also an accused in the Alipore Bomb Case.

7 The man who had shot Shamsul Alam.

8 Younger brother of Aurobindo Ghosh and chief accused in the Alipore Bomb Case.

9 Hem Chandra Das (Kanungo) of Midnapur went to Paris to learn the technique of manufacturing bombs; an accused in the Alipore Bomb Case.

10 Ullaskar Dutt is an important accused in the Alipore Bomb Case.

11 Avinash Bhattacharya is the Arbelia cousin of Naren Bhattacharya and one of the founders of *Jugantar* newspaper; accused in the Alipore Bomb Case.

12 King Emperor vs. Nani Gopal Gupta and others, "Calcutta Weekly Notes", *CWN*, Vol. XV, p. 596.

13 *C.W.N.*, Vol. XV, p. 597.

14 *Ibid.*: p. 597.

15 Interview with Alok Chakravarty.

16 Biman Behari Mazumdar: *Militant Nationalism in India*, pp. 110-11. Interviewed by the author, however, Purna Sen, an accused in the Alipore Bomb Case and belonging to the Midnapur Group of Satyen Bose, said that "Aurobindo had nothing to do with the murder. It was entirely Barin's idea".

17 M. N. Roy wrote: "Barin used to say that the worst of cowards could walk up to the gallows if he knew that the whole country was applauding. That remark made a deep impression on me; perhaps it was a pointer to the way of life I choose eventually." (Article on "Jatin Mukherjee", *Independent India*, 27th February 1949.)

# VII. The New Beginning

THE LIBERAL NATIONALIST LEADERS LED BY SURENDRA NATH
Banerjea had continued their efforts with the government
for the reversal of partition. Banerjea, assisted by Ambika
Charan Majumdar of Faridpore, had a memorial signed by
"representative men from 18 out of 25 Districts" of Bengal
and submitted it in June 1911 to the government for a
fresh consideration of the matter. However, the sudden
spate of terrorist-revolutionary activities in protest against
partition and the unearthing of the Manicktolla and Howrah
conspiracies had already caused rethinking among the British administrators about continuation of partition. In
fact, towards the end of 1910, the new Viceroy Hardinge,
and the Secretary of State, Crewe, "felt that the unrest in
India was chiefly due to the partition of Bengal, and there
would be no peace until the grievous wrong was remedied"[1].
The Government of India thus recommended the annulment of the partition of Bengal in its Despatch of 25th
August 1911. On 12th December of the same year the King
in his proclamation, ordered reunification of two Bengals
but shifted the capital of India to Delhi and transferred
some Bengali-speaking areas to Behar and Orissa.

The annulment of the partition was, no doubt, highly
welcome in Bengal and did satisfy a large section of Bengalis,
but it came too late to check the growth of militant nationalism which that measure had given birth to. The revolutionary movement in Bengal continued despite the conces-

51

sion and despite all the repressive measures of the government and the ban on revolutionary societies. This was in sharp contrast with Maharashtra where the government was able to suppress the revolutionary movement much sooner. One of the reasons for this was that in contrast with Maharashtra where the movement was primarily led by the Chitpavan Brahmins, the movement in Bengal was led and manned by the educated middle class irrespective of caste consideration[2] and by people who were younger in age.

On 23rd December 1912, two Bengalis, Rashbehari Bose and Basanta Kumar Biswas (who disguised himself as a Muslim lady in *purdah*) threw a bomb in an attempt to kill the Viceroy, Lord Hardinge, which resulted in the Delhi Conspiracy Case. Rashbehari Bose had close link with Amarendra Nath Chattopadhyaya of Uttarpara, and Basanta Biswas was sent to Rashbehari by Amarendra with the bomb which was manufactured in Chandernagore.[3] The Chandernagore centre was set up in 1910 by Amarendra and Motilal Roy.[4]

After his release from the Howrah Case, Naren went to stay at the residence of Saralabala Sarkar with Suresh Majumdar, his co-accused with whom he became very friendly in the jail. During his stay there, Naren decided to take up the garb of a *sadhu*-seeking religious man searching for *guru*. Sivnarain Swami was dead. So at this time he went to Benares as a *sadhu*-seeker in order to find out fugitives of the Sepoy Mutiny, if there were any, in the garb of *sadhus,* Naren wanted to gather knowledge about guerilla type warfare from these people to apply it to his plan for armed insurrection against the British.[5] He spent about three to four months in Benares and then returned to Calcutta where he continued his search for such *sadhus*. Recalling this period, Bhupati Mazumdar said, "Naren used to take me from one *sadhu* to another". Even Mazumdar believed that Naren had become deeply religious in those days and "was constantly searching for *sadhus* and *sanyasis*".[6] Naren built up this cover effectively because of the heavy responsibility that had fallen upon him to give final shape to the plan for guerilla warfare and to build up an effective united organisation of all revolutionary groups.

After his release from jail in the Howrah Conspiracy Case, Naren requested his elder brother, Sushil, to get him Rs. 300 for payment of his court expenses. Sushil and Naren mortgaged their house at Changripota to one Jatin Chakravarty[7] and soon thereafter they moved to a boarding house at 6 Mirzapur Street in Calcutta. Sushil's wife had died and there was no female member in the family, so they decided to move to the boarding house. The family, however, could not recover the Changripota house ever again.

Naren, however, rarely stayed with his brother after the Howrah Case and visited him only occasionally. Sushil knew about Naren's activities and always gave him cover and protection whenever he needed it. After his release from jail, Naren took up an employment—also as a cover—as agent of the "India Equitable Assurance Company".[8] He also worked as a Bill Collector of a rice mill and a timber works in Beliaghata.[9] In 1912-13, Naren mainly stayed at a boarding house in Sreegopal Mullick Lane. While there, he used to visit the Eden Hindu Hostel of the Presidency College and have his tea there with the students in the room of Satish Chakravarty, who was then an M.A. student. In the evening Naren and Jatin Mukherjee were frequent visitors to the Science Students' 'Mess' of the Calcutta University at 110, College Street. At this rendezvous those who came included the reputed scientists, Jnan Chandra Ghosh[10] (later Chairman of U.G.C.) and Meghnad Saha (of Saha Institute of Nuclear Physics). When M. N. Roy sent his emissary, Nalini Gupta, to India from Moscow in 1921, one of the persons he asked him to contact was Meghnad Saha.[11] Recalling a typical evening, Satish Chakravarty said: although academically not well-educated, Naren was regarded highly for his political thinking. Naren at this time, recalls Chakravarty, used to give vent to his ideas of what would be the type of government in free India, how the Calcutta Corporation, and even local bodies, would be run and emphasised on people's participation in such bodies for the welfare and upliftment of the community in general. Chakravarty added: such

53

thoughts were not in the minds of revolutionaries at that time who were primarily concerned with only how to teach the British rulers some lessons.[12]

Soon after their release, Naren and Jatin Mukherjee met Harikumar, Amarendra and others and began mobilising the different groups to form a federated organisation under the leadership of Jatin Mukherjee in pursuance of the plan for armed insurrection,—the strategy of which was tentatively made during their internment in the Howrah Case. In 1911, Jatin Mukherjee went to Brindaban for the second time to meet Jatindranath Banerjee (then Niralamba Swami) where the plan was finally approved.

After his release Naren also visited Aurobindo at Pondicherry for Aurobindo's support and cooperation to the plan. This effort to bring Aurobindo back into politics or at least to get his support failed even though Naren had argued with Aurobindo that they were only following the plan that the latter had proposed to Jatin Mukherjee in 1903. This had disappointed Naren.[13]

However, Aurobindo's refusal of support did not deter Naren and Jatin Mukherjee from carrying on the activities. In 1912 Bholanath Chatterjee was sent to Siam to make a general survey and make contacts there for future requirement. Meanwhile, as the Anushilan Samity had been banned, a National Reading Society was formed at Beadon Square and a physical culture centre was organised at the house of Jibantara Haldar at Jeletola.[14] Naren also began to meet different groups and people with the new plan.

In early April 1913, Naren convened a secret meeting at the Calcutta maidan of some leading members of the Calcutta Anushilan Samity. The meeting was held early in the evening. (In these meetings they used to sit around with a football and if any passerby or suspected police agent passed they talked about funds and players of the club to give the impression that members of a soccer club were talking about the problems of the club.) Initiating the discussion at this meeting, Naren said: "We have taken the vow not to sit idle until the country became free. The Anushilan Samity no longer exists. Does it mean we shall only sit and watch what is happening in the country and not do anything?."

The meeting was attended by Naren, Dr. Jadugopal Mukherjee, Aswini Roy, Bholanath Chatterjee and two others: [15]

| ASWINI ROY | |
|---|---|
| said: | "No, certainly not; but we need a leader. Where is the leader?" |
| NAREN: | "I have found the leader." |
| ASWINI ROY: | "Who is he?" |
| NAREN: | "He does not wish to be acquainted with you at the moment, or disclose his identity." |
| ASWINI ROY: | "Then who will give us order?" |
| NAREN: | "You will get his order from me." |
| ASWINI ROY: | "That means you are the leader." |

The meeting ended without taking any decision because Naren could not name the leader. There was voting in the end which showed even division; both Aswini Roy and Dr. Jadugopal Mukherjee voting against Naren's proposal.[16] Naren, however, could not divulge the name because he had specific instruction from Jatin Mukherjee not to disclose his name at that point. Aswini Roy added: "Had Naren told the name of the leader everybody would have accepted Jatinda as leader and Naren's proposal would have been accepted." But because he could not do that, it only delay-ed matters—until the Burdwan-Midnapur flood a few months later. The flood in the Damodar river in 1913, which swept parts of Burdwan and Midnapur Districts, provided a meeting ground for all the revolutionaries. And it was during the flood relief operations that the revolutionaries met and decided to give practical shape to the organisation of the revolutionary party.[17] Aswini Roy added: "After Naren had evolved a plan he used to go ahead with it rather ruth-lessly and almost fanatically. At that meeting we quarelled. But Naren behaved as friendly as ever when we met a few days later and he talked to me in a manner as if nothing had happened. I was amazed and at that time again he appeared to me a riddle."

After that meeting, Aswini Roy continued: "I was being asked by my friends to marry because the police was all the time after me and I was under their vigilant watch. My friends said marriage would do away with the constant chase of the police. Monoranjan Bhattacharya[18] (later a celebrated stage actor) asked me either to marry or to become a stage actor. Monoranjan argued that if I joined the professional stage, police would give me up as a spoiled young man. I had been thinking about it all the time when Naren saw me. He came to me and said: 'Aswini, you are a fool. Why don't you marry if that drives away the police?' and added 'for us marriage is nothing except another cover for our work'. "Aswini Roy remarked: "He was like an ancient Rishi—whose one objective was to achieve freedom of the Motherland and he never hesitated to do whatever was needed in pursuance of that objective and never flinched from his duty."[19]

Jatin Mukherjee believed in decentralised organisation unlike Naren, because Jatin Mukherjee thought that if one group was apprehended by the police and suppressed, then others could carry on the work unaffected. That is why he made it a rule that only leaders of groups should know each other, but none else; even the leaders of the groups should not try to ascertain who the members of other groups were nor try to meet them. The different groups should function in absolute secrecy. But when the idea of armed insurrection was conceived, Naren suggested that it was necessary to have a centralised organisation and leadership. But while Naren only argued on that point with Jatin Mukherjee, he scrupulously carried out Jatin Mukherjee's instructions to the point of making himself unpopular in many instances. But until Jatin Mukherjee had agreed he did not give vent to his ideas to any other person.

Thus, when Naren thought of uniting the groups, Jatin Mukherjee gave green signal to his enterprise but told him not to disclose his name. It was Naren's idea to build up such a unified organisation under Jatin Mukherjee's leadership because Naren knew that Jatin Mukherjee was probably the only person who could provide such a leadership.

Jatin Mukherjee, in his turn, realised the ability of Naren, who became the *de facto* leader, as most of the workers knew only Naren while Jatin Mukherjee continued to remain behind the scene. Besides, as Satish Chakravarty said, ". . . at that time the revolutionaries were so frustrated that all activities had almost ceased; it was Naren who, as the driving force, kept us all active and the organisation gradually began to function".[20]

Recounting this phase of Naren's work, Harikumar writes: "It is doubtful whether Jatindranath (Jatin Mukherjee) or the Jugantar group could achieve so much success and in such a short time without Naren", and adds, ". . . the organisation of the Jugantar group was the handiwork of Narendranath; Jatindranath gave it life and prestige and transformed it into an active political organisation".[21]

NOTES AND REFERENCES

[1] R. C. Majumdar: *History of Freedom Movement in India*, Vol. II, Firma K. L. Mukhopadhyaya, Calcutta, 1963, p. 263.

[2] Giving an account of age, caste and occupation of 186 Bengali revolutionaries convicted of specific outrages, conspiracy, etc. the Sedition Committee Report states 68 (31%) were students of whom 50 were below the age of 20. Most of the revolutionaries belonged to the age group 21 to 30, whose number was 105 (56%). Thus, 155 out of 186 (83%) were below the age of 30. Castewise, in Bengal there were 87 Kayasthas (46%) compared to 65 Brahmins (35%) and 13 Vaidyas (7%). By contrast, in Maharashtra, all the persons involved in the revolutionary movement were Brahmins and mostly Chitpavan Brahmins.

[3] Dr. Jadugopal: p. 301.

[4] *Ibid.*: p. 302.

[5] Interview with Alok Chakravarty.

[6] Interview with Bhupati Mazumdar, also corroborated by Phani Chakravarty's confession.

[7] Interview with Lalit Bhattacharya.

[8] Interview with Lalit Bhattacharya.

[9] Interview with Satish Chakravarty.

[10] Jnan Chandra Ghosh later told Dr. Bhupen Dutt in Germany that Jatin Mukherjee had told him that Naren Bhattacharya was his strong right arm [*vide*: Dr. Bhupendra Dutt's *Aprakasita Rajnaitik Itihas* (Unpublished Political History of India), p. 255.

[11] As told to me by Bhupendra Kumar Dutt.

[12] Interview with Satish Chakravarty.

[13] Interview with Nirvan Swami. Roy told Pundit Laxman Sastri Joshi, in the early 'forties, that he was disappointed after his meeting with Aurobindo. He had gone to Aurobindo to get the latter's support for the new plan (as told to me by Pundit Laxman Sastri Joshi).

[14] Interview with Jitendra Kumar Basu.

[15] Interview with Dr. Aswini Lal Roy.

[16] Interview with Dr. Aswini Lal Roy.

[17] Gobinda Lal Banerjee: *Dynamics of Revolutionary Movement in India*, p. 26.

[18] The celebrated stage actor.

[19] Interview with Dr. Aswini Lal Roy.

[20] Interview with Satish Chakravarty.

[21] Harikumar: p. 9.

# VIII. Preparation for Armed Insurrection

INDIAN REVOLUTIONARIES HAVE HELD THE VIEW THAT England's difficulty would be India's opportunity; and efforts were made to contact potential enemies of England to help Indian revolutionaries to wage guerilla type warfare for gaining independence of the country.

In 1906 after Jatindranath Banerjee fell out with Barin Ghosh he became a *sanyasi* and went to U.P. and Punjab and preached revolution there. He was able to convert Ajit Singh and his brother Kissen Singh (father of Bhagat Singh). Lala Hardayal, who went to study in England, returned in 1908, and became interested in the programme of the Bengal revolutionaries through Kissen Singh after his return. In 1911, Hardayal went to America and started a journal in the name of *Ghadr*[1] and established a centre in the name of "Jugantar Ashram".

After Hardayal's arrest in that country by the American Government on 16th March 1914, on charge of being an 'anarchist', he fled to Switzerland; and Ramchandra took charge of the Ashram and the journal. Pingle and Satyen Sen joined the group in San Francisco[2] at that time. Satyen Sen was sent to America by Jatin Mukherjee to make contacts with the Ghadr Party.[3]

In 1913, Hardayal told an Indian audience in America that "Germany was preparing to go to war with England and it is time for India to get ready for the coming revolution". The first scheme of the Ghadr Party was to send

59

the Sikhs from America to India and raise an insurrection. Later, the Ghadr Party and the Germans worked closely together with the "Indian Independence Committee" in Berlin acting as the liaison. Dhiren Sarkar (brother of Prof. B. K. Sarkar) sent information to the Bengal revolutionaries in 1913 that Germany could help the Indian revolutionaries if war broke out.[4]

On 6th March 1914, the *Berlinger Tageblatt* carried an article which said that the day of reckoning for England would come far sooner than officials dreamt of and added "there exists a real revolutionary climate". Especially in California there seems to have been an organised effort for the purpose of providing Indians with arms and explosives. Towards the end of 1913, Naren Bhattacharya began efforts to make contact with the Germans through the German Consulate-General in Calcutta; and by the beginning of 1914 this contact was made with the help of an important educationist in Calcutta. Satish Chakravarty, at the request of Naren, arranged this meeting with the German Consulate-General through D. Thibault, then Registrar of Calcutta University. Chakravarty told me that the better students of the University used to visit the house of Sir Ashutosh Mukherjee on Sundays where Thibault also used to come. Chakravarty told Thibault one day that some friends of his wanted to meet the German Consul-General to start business with Germany. On Satish Chakravarty's request Thibault arranged a meeting with the German Consul-General, not knowing who these friends were. Thereupon, Naren and Jatin Mukherjee met the German Consul-General. Naren and Jatin Mukherjee held several meetings with the German Consul-General in Calcutta by the beginning of 1914, to discuss plans for armed insurrection and guerilla warfare against the British power in India as soon as the war broke out and emphasised the need for arms aid from Germany. Some of these meetings were attended by Atul Krishna Ghosh, another close associate of Jatin Mukherjee.

At this point, Naren gave up his jobs and opened a restaurant near the office of Harry and Sons. The restaurant—where Naren cooked special dishes for sailors and soldiers—soon became a favourite spot for visiting sailors and soldiers and served as a centre for procurement of arms and exchange of information.[5]

Also in 1913 a great discontent arose amongst the Sikhs who had settled in Canada. The Sikhs were prevented by a Canadian Privy Council Order from bringing their wives and children into Canada. The Canadian order also stopped new Indian immigrants from going to Canada. Steamship companies also refused to accept bookings of Indians intending to go to Canada. One Gurudutt Singh, a businessman of Malay and Singapore, took up the challenge and chartered a Japanese ship, *Kamagatamaru,* and sailed for Canada with about 500 Sikh passengers from different places. The Ghadr Party contacted these men and distributed propaganda literatures to these people. The Sikhs were, however, not allowed to land in Canada from whence they came to Budge Budge near Calcutta on 29th September 1914.

The British Government in India decided to take these Sikhs in a sealed train to Bombay which the Sikhs refused and a gun fight ensued between the Sikhs and the government forces when the Government forced their landing in Calcutta. Many Sikhs were killed and many others were injured and admitted to the Medical College Hospital. Their leader Gurudutt Singh, however, managed to escape with 28 others and joined the Bengal revolutionaries. The Bengal revolutionaries actively helped the Sikhs at this time under the leadership of Satcori Banerjee, one of Naren's close associate in the Changripota group.

The impact of this incident upon revolutionary activity in India was tremendous and it revealed that men of the Ghadr Party and other Indians were procuring arms for the Indian revolution.

Soon after the declaration of war, Naren contacted the German Consul-General in Calcutta for a second series of meetings and information about the prospect of German help reached the Bengal group through the German Consul-General in Calcutta. Naren had already started meeting different groups to unite them in a federated party under the leadership of Jatin Mukherjee. About this time, Jatin Mukherjee was called to Calcutta. (After his release from the Howrah Conspiracy Case, Jatin Mukherjee, who lost his government job, had taken up the business of a contractor and mostly stayed outside of Calcutta except occasionally visiting the city to contact and advise his closest associates. During his visits to Calcutta, he used to stay at the residence of Atul Krishna Ghosh at 2 Chidam Mudi Lane in North Calcutta.)[6] At a hurriedly called secret meeting of the different revolutionary groups, Jatin Mukherjee was at this time elected the supreme leader of the united party;[7] no name was given to the party at this or any other time but the party decided to publish a bulletin in the name of *Jugantar* because the name had become popular.[8] The party, however, eventually came to be known as the Jugantar Party and the only group which did not join the Jugantar Party at this time was the Dacca Anushilan group, which had reservations about the feasibility of the plan for armed insurrection.

While Naren began his preparations for armed insurrection and Jatin Mukherjee fully endorsed the idea, Satish Sarkar (now Nirvan Swami) opposed the plan on the ground that "two major preconditions for guerilla warfare were absent". Satish Sarkar said that these preconditions were: "1. the ability of the revolutionaries to paralyse the transport and communication system and 2. existence of popular support to provide protection to the revolutionaries in times of need, particularly in the rural areas."[9] Satish Sarkar had once earlier stopped Jatin Mukherjee from making preparations for guerilla warfare by appealing to Niralamba Swami, the political guru of Jatin Mukherjee. But this time Naren argued that arrangements for paralysing railway transport and communication would be made and that when arms would be available it would be possible to organise a powerful revolutionary army to which people would extend the required support. On Naren's argument Jatin Mukherjee endorsed the plan and even obtained Niralamba Swami's support. Naren had also advanced the argument that the British forces in India would be so depleted at the time of the war that there would be very little British force left to resist the revolutionaries and all steps will be taken to stop reinforcements from being brought. The Indian troops, Naren said, would also come to the aid of the revolutionaries.[10]

Thereafter, Naren set himself at work. A cloth shop was opened at Chakradharpur on the Bengal Nagpur Railway and at a little distance from there another shop was opened by Bholanath Chatterjee, who had returned from Siam, as centres of coordination. In Balasore, Saileswar Bose opened a cycle shop under the name of Universal Emporium and a centre was set up at Sambalpur—all in preparation for the coming revolution, to paralyse the transport and communication system when necessary.

But while Jatin Mukherjee was called back to Calcutta, the firm arrangement for German arms had not yet been made. A meeting was then held in Calcutta where the plan for looting the arms of Rodda and Company was made. The meeting was arranged at midnight at a small park in Bowbazar near *Chhatawala Gali*, two days before the actual loot. The meeting was attended by Naren, Ashu Roy, Naren Ghosh Chaudhury, Sris Pal, Anukul Mukherjee, Haridas Dutt and Sris Mitra (Habul) who was an employee of the Company. Srish Mitra brought the information about the arrival of a stock of arms and the plan set up was as follows: Srish Mitra would deliver the goods to the revolutionaries who would bring a cart and the goods would then be taken to different secret places of the revolutionaries.

The Sedition Committee Report states: "On Wednesday, the 26th of August 1914, the clerk of Rodda and Company (Sris Mitra), whose duty it was to clear imports of arms and ammunition at the Custom Office, had cleared 202 cases of arms and ammunition, but had brought only 192 cases to his employer's warehouse in Vansittart Row. He had then left, saying that he was going to bring the remainder. He never returned and after three days the case was reported to the police. The 10 missing cases contained 50 Mauser

63

pistols and 46,000 rounds of Mauser ammunition for the same, the pistols were of large size, 0.360 bore .... The pistols were so constructed and packed that by attaching to the butt the box containing the pistols, a weapon was produced which could be fired from the shoulder in the same way as a rifle."[11]   Out of 50 pistols, 25 were taken to 9 Jagadish Nath Roy Lane where Atul Krishna Ghosh's nephew lived[12] and the other half hidden in a temple at Khardah where the priest of Atul Krishna Ghosh was in charge.[13]  As the police became active the stock from the temple was removed by Naren to another place. Because of the Anushilan Samity's opposition to the plan for armed insurrection the cleavage between Jugantar and Anushilan had increased so much by this time that the Anushilan Samity Secretary, Pulin Mukherjee, refused to help the revolutionaries to hide these arms and ammunitions.[14] Naren became the big target of the Anushilan Samity's attack because he was the main sponsor of the plan as well as of the Jugantar Party.  In fact when Pulin Mukherjee heard that Naren was involved in the looting he made a blithering attack on Naren to Amar Krishna Ghosh, younger brother of Atul Krishna Ghosh, who was sent with the request for help.[15]

These Mauser pistols came to be very useful as the group had to resort mainly to dacoities for fund raising.  Besides, the weapons would also be useful in time of the planned insurrection.  They were, therefore, distributed to various centres. According to the Sedition Committee Report: "44 of these pistols were almost at once distributed to 9 different revolutionary groups in Bengal and it is almost certain that the pistols so distributed were used in 54 cases of dacoity or murder or attempts at dacoity or murder subsequent to August 1914."[16]

One day, when Naren was staying on the second floor of the Sree Gouranga Press building of Suresh Mazumdar, with two Mauser pistols on the table and a map of the Sunderbans there was a knock at the door.  Naren and Suresh were surprised but Naren asked Suresh to open the door and placed a newspaper over the pistols. Tegart, the sharpest of the police officers in those days entered the room.

But unperturbed Naren talked with Tegart for about half an hour. Tegart returned apparently convinced that no revolution was being planned there and the men were only busy with their printing business.

In November 1914, Satyen Sen returned to Calcutta. On his way back he had met Sun Yat Sen, the Chinese national-ist leader. Satyen Sen found Pingle and a large number of Sikhs travelling in the same ship. Reaching Calcutta, Satyen Sen introduced Pingle and the leader of the Sikhs, Kartar Singh, to Naren and Jatin Mukherjee who sent them to Rashbehari Bose. Pingle assured them that 4,000 men had come from America for the purpose of the revo-lution and 20,000 more would come when the rebellion would begin.[17]

After the Delhi Conspiracy Case, Rashbehari had been living in Benares. At this point, he decided to accompany Pingle to Lahore and "sent for Jatin Mukherjee and Naren Bhattacharya" at Benares.[18] Soon after, Rashbehari, Jatin Mukherjee, Amarendra Nath Chattopadhyaya, Atul Krishna Ghosh and Naren Bhattacharya met at Benares and discuss-ed the plan for armed insurrection. At this meeting Jatin Mukherjee took charge of Bengal and Rashbehari of U.P. and the Punjab; and 21st February 1915 was decided as the date for the uprising.[19]

It was decided that Rashbehari would hold the Down Punjab Mail at Amritsar and that would be the signal for the uprising. That would indicate that it has started in the Punjab. Accordingly, the Bengal group renewed con-tact with the army at the Fort William in Calcutta. (In Maharashtra an organisation was set up by Benoy Bhusan Dutt, Bhim Rao and Dr. Savarkar, brother of Veer Savarkar, who had been a student of the Medical College in Calcutta.) Another connection was established with Punjab through Ashutosh Ghosh, a school teacher in case the link with Rash-behari was snapped.[20]

A series of dacoities was now planned and executed in Calcutta by Naren and others because Jatin Mukherjee wanted one lakh of rupees for the execution of the plan for insurrection. The job of raising this fund was entrusted to Naren.[21] To those who objected to the dacoities at Calcutta at this time Jatin Mukherjee argued that these would damage the prestige of the government in Calcutta. He added that one action in Calcutta is equal to 10 actions in the rural areas from propaganda point of view.[22]

## GARDEN REACH DACOITY

On the 12th February 1915 Naren with two others looted the cash of Bird and Company in broad daylight in Garden Reach at Calcutta, in the first dacoity of the series. This dacoity which has come to be known as the Garden Reach Political Dacoity created a sensation at Calcutta. This was the first motor dacoity and the whole operation was completed within a few minutes at gun point without having to fire a shot.

This was followed by similar motor dacoities at Beliaghata (22nd February), Corporation Street (now Surendra Nath Banerjee Street), Grey Street, Talla and Armenian Street in quick succession.[23]

The Garden Reach dacoity alone brought Rs. 18,000 to the revolutionaries. It was arranged that Naren would go to Jatin Mukherjee personally and inform him about the dacoity's success and hand over to him the money, the next day. On the next day, Jatin Mukherjee was waiting for Naren in the house of Dwarkanath Vidyabhusan at Mirzapur Street, where Phani Chakravarty lived. But Naren failed to turn up even long after the appointed hour. Jatin Mukherjee was upset, then Bipin Ganguly came and told him "Naren was coming in a round about way" to hoodwink the police. After a while news came that while crossing Kantapukur Lane, Naren had fallen in the hands of the police. Inspector Suresh Mukherjee was able to apprehend him.

Jatin Mukherjee was so upset by the news that he walked over to the house of Dr. Jadugopal Mukherjee (this was the first time that Dr. Jadugopal Mukherjee said he and Jatin Mukherjee really met each other) and told him "my right arm has been broken".[24] Jatin Mukherjee then wanted to attack the Lall Bazar Police Headquarters immediately to bring Naren out of jail. A suggestion was then made to rescue him from the prison van when he would be taken to the Police Court from Lall Bazar on the next day. Arrangements for Mauser pistols were made and five selected volunteers were sent to carry out the job. These included Gopen Roy, Satish Chakravarty, Prof. Ludli Mitter and two others.[25] But Naren fell ill inside the jail and was not taken to the court that day.

At this point, Dr. Jadugopal Mukherjee suggested that efforts should be made to get bail for Naren. Without taking any chances Jatin Mukherjee himself went to the Chief Government Pleader, Tarak Sadhu, for his advice. The need to get Naren out of jail was so great that Jatin Mukherjee despite being in hiding, took the risk of approaching the Government Pleader for favour and advice. Tarak Sadhu was respectful towards Jatin Mukherjee and told him that if any one of the group could come forward and make a confession that he was responsible for the dacoity, then Naren could be given bail. Accordingly, Jatin Mukherjee sent a note (a note written in his own hands) to Purna Das, leader of the Faridpur Group, requesting him to arrange for such a volunteer to accept the responsibility for the dacoity. On Purna Das's request, Radhacharan Pramanick, one of those who had accompanied Naren in the dacoity, signed such a statement and Naren was given bail. Radhacharan Pramanick was given seven years, rigorous imprisonment in the case and died in an insane condition during the jail term.[26]

Naren was released on bail for Rs. 1,000 with two sureties on 22nd February 1915.[27] After obtaining bail, Naren walked straight to the house of Jitendra Kumar Basu, nephew of Atul Krishna Ghosh, at 9 Jagadish Nath Roy Lane, and borrowing Rs. 200 from him walked to the house of his younger sister, Pannamoyee, at Tarak Pramanick Lane and went into hiding the same evening.

Inspector Suresh Mukherjee, who had apprehended Naren, was shot dead on 28th February near the Cornwallis Square in North Calcutta under Jatin Mukherjee's order.[28]

Rashbehari had in the meantime advanced the date of insurrection from 21st to 19th February suspecting leakage of information to the police. The plan for insurrection on the 19th February had failed however because of betrayal by one Kripal Singh, who had cleverly enrolled himself in Rashbehari's party. Rashbehari trusted him because he had come from Shanghai as a Ghadr Party worker. The change of the date was also leaked to the government by Kripal Singh,[29] which led to the final miscarriage of the plot.

Thirteen of the revolutionaries were arrested in Lahore with arms and ammunitions, literature and four flags of their design.[30] Rashbehari and Pingle escaped even though Kripal Singh tried to get them arrested. Kartar Singh and some others were arrested and they were tried and sentenced in the Lahore Conspiracy Case. Kartar Singh was hanged.

Rashbehari fled to Benares. From there he came to Bengal and finally left for Japan on 12th May 1915 under the assumed name of P. N. Tagore.[31] Pingle, however, continued his work among the troops and was arrested on 23rd March from the lines of the 12th Indian Cavalry with a tin box containing ten bombs. Some Indian soldiers and Pingle were arrested and Pingle was hanged to death.

### NOTES AND REFERENCES

[1] Dr. Jadugopal: p. 31.

[2] Dr. Jadugopal: pp. 30-31.

[3] Prithwin Mukherjee's serialised biography of Jatin Mukherjee in *Basumati* (Weekly), p. 1245.

[4] Dr. Jadugopal: p. 421.

[5] Interview with Alok Chakravarty.

[6] Interview with Nalini Kar.

[7] M. N. Roy writes in his Memoirs "Clandestine Conferences led to the formation of the General Staff of the coming revolution, with Jatin Mukherjee as the Commander-in-Chief". (*Memoirs*, p. 3.)

[8] Interview with Dr. Jadugopal Mukherjee.

[9] Interview with Nirvan Swami.

[10] Interview with Nirvan Swami.

[11] *Sedition Committee Report*, p. 66.

[12] Interview with Jitendra Kumar Basu.

13 Interview with **Amar Krishna Ghosh.**

14 *Ibid.*

15 *Ibid.*

16 *Sedition Committee Report*, p. 66.

17 B. B. Mazumdar: *Militant Nationalism in India*, p. 167.

18 Dr. Jadugopal: p. 393.

19 *Ibid.*: p. 384.

20 *Ibid.*: p. 385.

21 M. N. Roy writes in his Memoirs: "The job of finding money for initial expenditure, entrusted to me, was soon done according to plan." (*Memoirs*, p. 3.)

In the late 'thirties, while appealing for funds for his Weekly, *Independent India*, M. N. Roy told his followers that Jatinda merely expressed the wish that he needed one lakh of rupees and "we immediately set out to get the funds and gave him more than what he wanted". He lamented that this idealism was lacking in the generation of the 'thirties.

22 Interview with Dr. Jadugopal Mukherjee.

23 Dr. Jadugopal: p. 386.

24 Interview with Dr. Jadugopal Mukherjee.

25 Interview with Satish Chakravarty.

26 Interview with Kali Prasad Banerjee (Faridpur group) and confirmed by Dr. Jadugopal Mukherjee.

27 The two mukhtears who forfeited their bail amounts were reimbursed by the group. The two mukhtears were Kali Prasanna Chatterjee and Sashi Bhusan Das (as told to me by Kali Charan Ghosh).

28 Interview with Jitendra Kumar Basu.

29 B. B. Majumdar: *Militant Nationalism in India*, p. 169.

30 *Ibid.*: p. 169.

31 Dr. Jadugopal: p. 387.

# IX. From Balasore to Batavia

ON FEBRUARY 22ND 1915, WHILE JATIN MUKHERJEE, NAREN Bhattacharya and others were holding a secret meeting at a house in Pathuriaghata Street, a police Sub-Inspector, Nirode Haldar, suddenly appeared in the room where they were meeting and asked if Naren was there. Inside the room he saw Jatin Mukherjee and cried out: "Jatin Babu what are you doing here?" He was immediately shot dead and the group left that place immediately and went to another secret hideout in Haritaki Bagan Lane. It was then felt unsafe to keep Jatin Mukherjee in Calcutta any more. Naren then went to Mohandia village to find out a secret hideout for Jatin Mukherjee. Nalini Kar who had once absconded in this place went with Naren to show him the place. Naren approved of the place and then Jatin Mukherjee was removed there with three armed guards of the Faridpur group and Nalini Kar.[1] The Universal Emporium at Balasore was to be the link between Jatin Mukherjee's hideout and Calcutta, and Nalini Kar was to commute between Calcutta and Jatin Mukherjee's hideout.

Shortly after Jatin Mukherjee was removed to Mohandia, Jiten Lahiri brought information from Germany to the Bengal revolutionaries in March 1915 that two ship loads of arms and ammunition were being sent from America. Heramba Gupta, with the help of the Germans in America, also arranged to send a trained military man, George Paul Boehm, to give military training to the Indians in Burma

70

so that Indians could liberate Burma, which was still a province of India, with the help of the Indian army and the police. This would be followed by an attack on Bengal by the Indians of Siam and Burma.[2] It was also arranged that the Ghadr Party members would raise a revolt in the Punjab villages and within the army.[3]

The Germans then asked the Bengal revolutionaries to send a representative to Batavia to work out the details of the plan and accordingly, Naren was sent to Batavia in April 1915, under the adopted name of C. Martin, as an agent of Harry and Sons.[4] The link between Calcutta and Batavia was maintained through Harry and Sons with its office at 41 Clive Street. It also acted as the link between Naren Bhattacharya and others[5] and the revolutionaries obtained their instructions from Harry and Sons and gave informations there.[6]

On his arrival at Batavia, Martin was introduced by the German Consul-General to Theodore Helfferich, a big German businessman in Java.[7] Helfferich told him that a ship load of arms and ammunitions was on its way to Karachi to assist the Indians in their revolution. "Martin" then urged that the ship should be diverted to Bengal. This was agreed upon after reference to the German Consul-General in Shanghai. Martin then telegraphed Harry and Sons in Calcutta that "business was helpful". In June, Harry and Sons cabled Martin for money and thereafter began a series of remittances from Helfferich in Batavia to Harry and Sons in Calcutta. Between June and August, these remittances, according to the Sedition Committee Report, totalled about Rs. 43,000 out of which the revolutionaries were able to withdraw about Rs. 33,000 before the government discovered the conspiracy.

In the middle of June, Martin returned to India making arrangements to receive the cargo of S.S. *Maverick*, as the ship was called, at Rai Mangal, in the Sunderbans in southern Bengal. The cargo was reported to consist of 30,000 rifles with 400 rounds of ammunition for each and two lakhs of rupees in cash.

After his return from Batavia, Naren went straight to

71

Mohandia to discuss with Jatin Mukherjee the plan to receive the cargo of Maverick and employ it to the best advantage. Those who were consulted in the plan included Atul Krishna Ghosh, Dr. Jadugopal Mukherjee, Bholanath Chatterjee, Harikumar Chakravarty and a few others.

They decided to divide the arms into three parts, viz. (1) Hatiya, for the East Bengal Districts in the charge of the Barisal group: Naren Ghosh Choudhury, Monoranjan Gupta and others were sent there; (2) Calcutta: this would be in the charge of Naren Bhattacharya himself and Bipin Ganguly. They had received assurances of collaboration from the soldiers in the Fort William at Calcutta and planned to raid all the ammunition shops before capturing Calcutta. The task for blowing up any bridge or building, if necessary was given to Phani Chakravarty, Bhupati Mazumdar and Brajen Dutt; and (3) Balasore: Jatin Mukherjee himself would remain in charge in Balasore.[8]

The revolutionaries based their calculations for insurrection on Naren's argument that the British authorities would be compelled to send out the major portion of their forces stationed in India. For several weeks, in fact, before the arrival of some untrained territorial battalions from England the total British garrison in India was reduced to less than 15,000 men.[9] Within the first few weeks of the war, the Indian Government sent out (of the country) in all 80,000 British Officers and troops and 210,000 Indian officers and men, together with 70 million rounds of small arms and ammunition, 60,000 rifles and more than 550 guns of the latest type.[10]

The revolutionaries thus considered that they were numerically strong enough to deal with the troops in Bengal, although they apprehended reinforcement from outside. Hence they planned to hold up the three main railways to Bengal by blowing up the bridges. Jatin Mukherjee himself was to deal with the Madras Railways from Balasore, Bholanath Chatterjee was to take charge of the Bengal Nagpur Railway and Satish Chakravarty was to go to Burdwan to blow up the bridge on the East Indian Railway over the river Ajoy.[11] Naren Ghosh Choudhury and Phani Chakravarty were told to go to Hatiya where a force was to collect first to gain control of the Eastern Bengal Districts and then to march on to Calcutta. The Calcutta Party under Naren and Bipin Ganguly was to first take possession of all the arms and ammunition, then to capture Fort William[12] and afterwards take over the town of Calcutta. After the failure of the February (21/19) uprising, however, the government began to receive warning information of the projected uprising in Bengal,[13] with the help of German arms.

## THE FATE OF MAVERICK

S.S. *Maverick,* an oil tanker, which belonged to the German firm of F. Jebsen and Company of San Francisco, sailed from San Pedro, near Los Angeles, about 22nd April 1915. The ship first went to San Jos del Caleo, at the southernmost point of lower California, where a fresh clearance was obtained in very general terms for Java via the Pacific.

The ship then sailed for Socorro, a lonely island off the coast of Mexico where she was to meet a schooner named *Annie Larsen.* The schooner was to bring the cargo of arms from Acapulco in Mexico and these were to be transferred to *Maverick.* The rifles were to be stowed away in one of the oil tanks and flooded with oil, and the ammunition was to be stowed in another tank and flooded only in case of emergency.[14]

From four castaways who happened to be on the island, the captain of the *Maverick* learned that *Annie Larsen* had been there but being short of water and supplies had returned to the coast of Mexico. The captain received a note left for him by *Annie Larsen,* asking him to wait for her return.

The schooner *Annie Larsen* did not appear, and after waiting for 29 days, the captain of the ship, *Maverick,* decided to proceed to San Diego, California. At San Diego, he received instructions from his German owners to proceed to Hilo, in the Hawaii, for further orders. *Maverick* arrived in Hilo about 14th June and there received instruction from the captain of another German ship to proceed to Johnston island, a remote spot in south-west Hawaii and wait for *Annie Larsen*. However, when the ship arrived there the local press reported the entire plan in its War Bulletin—probably because some of the ship's crew composed of Ghadr Party men "talked too much" and may have leaked out the whole plot.[15]

After a fortnight's stay, *Maverick* was asked to proceed on her voyage to Java, after calling at Johnston island, but without any expectation of meeting *Annie Larsen*. Probably at this point the whole plan was abandoned.[16]

While the *Maverick* was at Socorro, the island was visited by H.M.S. *Kent* and H.M.S. *Rainbow* both of which sent in search parties on board. When the *Kent* first appeared, Hari Singh, the leader of the five-member Ghadr Party workers— they had posed themselves as Persians—who called himself Jehangir, had the papers and pamphlets burned in the engine room and thrown into the sea. When the *Maverick* reached Java, the Dutch Government searched it but found nothing. According to a Singapore newspaper report, the arms that were in the ship had also been thrown into the sea along with the Ghadr Party literatures.

In Batavia, Helfferich took charge of the ship and when later Martin went to America, he boarded the *Maverick* in place of Hari Singh.

## ANOTHER ATTEMPT TO SEND ARMS

Another attempt was made to send arms by the ship *Henry S,* a schooner with auxiliary crew. It cleared from Manila for Pontianak, on the west coast of Borneo, about 14th July 1915. The papers of *Henry S* was originally made out for Shanghai, and she had a consignment of arms and ammunition on board. These were, however, discovered by the Customs authorities and had to be taken off before she was allowed to leave Manila.

On 27th September, the German, American on board *Henry S,* George Paul Boehm, was arrested at Singapore while on his way from Batavia to Shanghai. In March, Boehm was introduced to Heramba Lal Gupta, a representative of the Bengal group in Chicago, Gupta told him that India was in a state of revolt and that a cargo of arms and ammunition had already left Mexico for India, and asked him if he could give training to Indians in Burma. Boehm agreed for 1,500 dollars to go to the Burmese frontier via Bangkok where the training was to take place. Boehm later met Jodh Singh and a Dutch-American named Sterneck. After receiving the agreed sum from the German Consulate, Boehm set off for Bangkok with Sterneck. After his arrival in Manila (in June 1915) Boehm called on the German Consul but was surprised to learn that the latter had no information about the plan. The letter which the German Consul was to have received seems to have gone astray.[17] It was this letter which the French authorities had intercepted and handed over to the English.

However, the German Consul instructed Boehm to sail on the *Henry S* and land about 500 out of the stock of 5,000 revolvers in the ship at Bangkok and take the rest to Chittagong.[18] But the plan was so badly coordinated that the whole project fizzled out.

<h2 style="text-align:center">NOTES AND REFERENCES</h2>

[1] Interview with Nalini Kar.

[2] Dr. Jadugopal: p. 33.

[3] *Ibid*: p. 34.

[4] Harikumar Chakravarty was an employee of the firm and the owner, Haridas Bhattacharya, agreed to lend the use of the firm for revolutionary work. The owner also belonged to Changripota.

[5] Dr. Jadugopal: p. 389.

[6] Interview with Dr. Aswini Lal Roy.

[7] Theodore Helfferich was manager of the German firm, Behn Mayers Company at Batavia. Theodore, with his brother Envil, was working in close collaboration with the German Consul and was the head of the Batavia centre of Indo-German conspiracy.

[8] Dr. Jadugopal: p. 35.

[9] Lord Hardinge: *My Indian Years*, pp. 102-03.

[10] B. B. Majumdar: *Militant Nationalism in India*, pp. 157-58.

[11] Interviewed by the author, Satish Chakravarty denied, however, that there was any plan for him to go to blow up the bridge at Ajoy. He thinks the Sedition Committee Report from where the information is taken is only partly correct. He added that the part relating to Jatin Mukherjee

was entirely wrong. Only Bholanath Chatterjee was deputed for the task if needed.

This portion of the Sedition Committee Report was almost entirely quoted from Phani Chakravarty's confession—SNR.

12 *Sedition Committee Report*, p. 83.

13 Lord Hardinge: *My Indian Years*, p. 118.

14 *Sedition Committee Report*, pp. 123-24.

15 According to B. B. Majumdar, the secret about the voyage of *Maverick* and *Annie Larsen* was leaked out through Kumud Nath Mukherjee, who was acting as a representative of the group in Siam, where he was a practising lawyer. (*Militant Nationalism in India*, p. 172.)

16 James Campbell Ker: *Political Trouble in India (1907-1917)*, pp. 272-73.

17 *Ibid.*: p. 274.

18 Dr. Jadugopal: p. 38.

# X. Trips to Batavia

BEFORE LEAVING FOR BATAVIA, NAREN HAD SET UP TWO TRAIN-
ing centres in Kidderpore in south Calcutta; one for training in signalling and telegraphy, and the other for guerilla
technique.[1] Volunteers were recruited and the centres were
run in such secrecy that the police had no knowledge of
these centres and even the Sedition Committee Report does
not mention it. About 50 boys stayed there all the time for
training and the camps were in charge of one Panchu
Gopal Banerjee (alias Panchkori Banerjee). The communication route to the centres was established through Howrah
by ferrying across the river, Hooghly.[2]

Naren stayed mostly in his own secret hideout at Haritaki
Bagan Lane in north Calcutta and sometimes in Bhowani-
pore, another hideout, in south Calcutta. These places were
known only to Dr. Jadugopal Mukherjee and Atul Krishna
Ghosh.[3] At regular intervals, he visited the training centres
and also went to Jatin Mukherjee at the latter's hideout at
Mohandia near Balasore for discussion. Before leaving for
Batavia, Naren went to Mohandia and discussed his plans
with Jatin Mukherjee.

Naren left for Batavia in April 1915 and boarded the
ship at Madras. Arriving at Batavia, he met the two Helfferichs and the German Consul and arranged, amongst
other things, for money to be sent to India. He cabled as
"C. A. Martin" to Harry and Sons at Calcutta and gave to
the people in Batavia the address of Harry and Sons and

77

some others, including Sramajibi Samabaya, for the use in future communications. Amarendra Nath Chattopadhyaya's Sramajibi Samabaya was to be used for communication with Naren only.[4] After finalising the agreement for arms, Naren returned to India in June, arriving at Megapatam on the 14th June. The next day he was in Madras and there he attempted to cash a Batavia remittance which he brought with him, a Bank draft in favour of "C. A. Martin or bearer". As the bank to which he submitted the cheque had not yet received the necessary advice from Batavia, payment was refused; the draft was later cashed in Calcutta by Amarendra Nath Chattopadhyaya. The remittances of German money from Java were arranged by Abdul Salam, a Kashmiri Mohammedan residing in Batavia, who forwarded them through a firm of Sindhi merchants trading widely in the Far East named, Chotirmall and Company. Abdul Salam was in the plot, and was later interned by the Government of Dutch East Indies.[5]

On his arrival at Madras, Martin sent the following telegram to Dr. Jadugopal Mukherjee at Calcutta "Arrived here starting tonight for Balasore expect to meet someone there". The discovery, later, that this telegram was sent led to enquiries at Balasore and finally resulted in the police search at Mohandia and the heroic battle between the police and Jatin Mukherjee at Kaptipoda in which the latter died. After meeting Jatin Mukherjee, Naren went on to Calcutta and got in touch with Kumud Nath Mukherjee who had come from Batavia with messages.

Kumud Nath Mukherjee was a Bengali who had been living in Bangkok since March 1912 where he practised as a lawyer. In April 1914 he met Bholanath Chatterjee and learned that the latter was connected with the revolutionaries in Bengal. Bholanath returned to Calcutta soon after the war broke out, and when the German scheme materialised he mentioned Kumud Nath Mukherjee to the Calcutta group as one of the sympathisers in Bangkok. Accordingly, in June 1915, he was approached by members of the Ghadr Party in Bangkok to take money and a message to Calcutta, and on the 18th June he left Bangkok with a sum supplied by Shiv Dayal Kapur. He reached Calcutta on the 3rd July and went to see Dr. Jadugopal Mukherjee as he was instructed to. And at Dr. Jadugopal's house, he also saw Bholanath. In Calcutta Kumud Nath Mukherjee was introduced to Naren by Bholanath as "the leader" but Naren's name was withheld from him.[6] Naren asked Kumud Nath to return to Batavia and deliver a message to Helfferichs explaining the continuing want of the revolutionaries in rifles and trained German help. Accordingly, Kumud Nath left India on the 24th July via Madras and carried out his mission.

After waiting for well over a fortnight at Raimangal in the Sunderbans, Dr. Aswini Roy and Satcori Banerjee returned to Calcutta and reported at Harry and Sons that no ship was seen. They were told about the special lights that the ship would carry—three lights in a row horizontally—and given the instruction that as soon as they would see the ship they should give the same light signal and receive the cargo of the ship when she came to the shore. They waited on a tree top by rotation and returned when nothing was seen for over 15 days beyond the expected date of arrival[7] of the ship.

Meanwhile, the *Maverick* had been searched and the arrangement for sending arms had been upset. The Penang newspaper article disclosing the whole plot was sent by Kumud Nath Mukherjee to Dr. Jadugopal Mukherjee in Calcutta who in turn transmitted the same to Jatin Mukherjee at Mohandia. On the 7th August, the police searched the office of Harry and Sons on suspicion of links with Batavia; Harikumar Chakravarty and his brother were arrested and all the papers seized.

About this time Naren decided to make his second trip to Batavia. Even though he "smelt" danger, Naren talked with Dr. Jadugopal Mukherjee about sending of arms by land route through North Eastern Frontier territory in Assam and went to Mohandia taking Phani Chakravarty with him. He wanted to take Phani Chakravarty along with him to Batavia and sought Jatin Mukherjee's approval. Naren spent two or three days in Mohandia and then left for

Batavia in the latter part of August, taking Phani Chakravarty with him. Phani Chakravarty was given the name,
"W. A. Payne". Accordingly, Dr. Jadugopal Mukherjee went
to N.E.F.A. with a group of revolutionaries.

After the search of Harry and Sons, police found papers
to show that the Universal Emporium at Balasore was a
subsidy of Harry and Sons, and proceeded to search the
Universal Emporium at Balasore. When the police party
came, Saileswar Bose was unable to explain some of the
papers. Saileswar's activities attracted the attention of the
police resulting in further search. Further searches revealed
that he visited a remote village in Mayurbhanj State called
Mohandia, 22 miles west of Balasore, right inside the jungle.
This was an unusual place for a Bengali of his class to go
and hence increased the suspicion of the police. On the
6th September, the District Magistrate of Balasore, accompanied by several police officers, engaged in the enquiry,
went to Mohandia and came to know that "several Bengalis
were living in a house in the jungle about a mile and a
half away". Next morning they searched the house but
Jatin Mukherjee and his armed escorts were all gone. They
had, however, left behind some papers among which were
a map of the Sunderbans and the cutting from the Penang
newspaper about *Maverick*.

On the 9th September, the District Magistrate of
Balasore received information that the group had been
located in the adjoining village, Kaptipoda, and had shot
one villager dead and wounded another. The Magistrate
with a party of armed police went to the spot and found
that Jatin Mukherjee and the group had taken refuge in
a small island of the jungle in the middle of the rice field.
As they approached, Jatin Mukherjee opened fire with
Mauser pistols. The fire was returned and for about 20
minutes the gun duel continued. Jatin Mukherjee had lost
or misplaced the key to the bag which contained the cartridges. He also received injury on one hand. At this point
two men from Jatin Mukherjee's party held up their hands
in token of surrender. The police party then advanced
across the mud and water and found that the group con-

sisted of five persons, of whom one was dead and two seriously injured. The dead man proved to be Jatin Mukherjee. One of the wounded, who died shortly afterwards, was Chittapriya Roy Choudhury of Faridpur group, who had assassinated Inspector Suresh Mukherjee.

The police discovered that the group had changed their names and adopted the names of the heroes of Bankim Chandra's novel, *Ananda Math,* while staying in Mohandia. Their abode in the jungle was intended to be the centre of a revolutionary band of *Children of the Mother.*[8] In the autumn of 1915, while passing through Manila, Naren "received the shocking news of Jatin Mukherjee's death". Naren had promised Jatin Mukherjee, "I shall not return without arms". His immediate resolve was that "Jatinda's death must be avenged". He travelled through the entire South-East Asia to find arms for the Indian revolution and avenge Jatinda's death.

## NOTES AND REFERENCES

[1] Interview with Nalini Kar and Satish Chakravarty.
[2] Interviews with Nalini Kar and Satish Chakravarty.
[3] Interview with Nalini Kar.
[4] Interview with Dr. Aswini Lal Roy.
[5] James Campbell Ker, *Political Trouble in India (1907-1917),* p. 278.
[6] *Ibid.*: p. 281.
[7] Interview with Dr. Aswini Lal Roy.
[8] James Campbell Ker, *Political Trouble in India (1907-1917),* p. 280.

F

# XI. In Search of Arms

THE ATTEMPT TO SMUGGLE ARMS BY SHIPS HAVING FAILED, Naren went to Batavia for the second time with an alternative plan of bringing them overland. They were to be smuggled through the North-Eastern tribal area, where the Abors, a major tribal population of N.E.F.A. in Assam, had risen in revolt only recently. Soon after he left for Batavia, a group of revolutionaries, led by Dr. Jadugopal Mukherjee, went to the North-Eastern Frontier areas. They were to incite the Abors and the neighbouring tribes to rise again in revolt, this time to be helped with arms and other resources, and the revolutionaries planned to lead this movement into the heartland of India to help the liberation of the country.

The next day after their arrival in Batavia, Naren went to Helfferich's house and met one of the Helfferichs and the German Consul. The latter listened to Naren but was apparently disillusioned now about the scheme. Helfferich told Naren that the scheme he spoke about now to send arms by land route through the North-Eastern Frontier was "an impossible one". Naren had three or four meetings with the Germans but evidently made little progress on his new mission.[1]

Naren made yet another attempt to bring help by overseas from Indonesia. The plan was to use the German ships interned at a port at the northern tip of Sumatra, to storm the Andaman islands and free and arm the prisoners, and form an army of liberation with the prisoners and land the army on the Orissa coast. The ships were armoured and carried several guns each. The crew of the ships were composed of naval ratings, and could assist in the aggression. Several hundred rifles and other small arms and an adequate quantity of ammunition, Naren planned to obtain through Chinese smugglers. But the Germans were unwilling to play the game. At the last moment the money for the purchase of arms was not forthcoming, and the plan miscarried. The German Consul-General "mysteriously disappeared" on the day when he was to issue orders for the purchase of arms.

Naren was getting restive and rather frustrated when he decided to go to Japan. He managed, however, to extract a fairly large sum of money from the Germans and remit the same to his comrades in India. Reaching Japan, Naren contacted Rashbehari Bose, his former comrade in India, who was already in Japan. Naren went to Japan with the hope that Rashbehari would help him, but was soon disappointed because Rashbehari's attitude had changed in the meantime. Rashbehari now believed in the liberating mission of Japan in Asia, and Naren, still a full-blooded nationalist revolutionary, was not convinced and not prepared to sacrifice India's cause for any other country. Japan was an ally of Britain in the war and Naren was sceptical about getting any help from that country. Besides, he could not afford to wait until Japan had won the war. His comrades were waiting "neither safe nor comfortable" in the North-Eastern tribal regions of Assam.

Naren left Rashbehari and met the Chinese nationalist leader Sun Yat-Sen, who had taken refuge in Japan following the defeat of the July 1913 uprising of Nanking. However, Sun Yat-Sen also believed in the liberating mission of Japan.

About the end of 1915, the Chinese provinces of Yunan and Szechuan were in revolt against Yuan Shi-Kai's plan to restore monarchy with himself as the Emperor. Naren thought that the inspiration for this revolt had come from Sun Yat-Sen and hence suggested to the latter that a political alliance of the Chinese and Indian peoples in their common struggle for freedom could be achieved if some arms from these two Chinese provinces bordering India and Burma were passed to the Indian revolutionaries across the border. Sun Yat-Sen suggested instead that Martin should approach the German Ambassador in Peking with the demand for five million dollars so that the entire store of arms and ammunitions in the hands of the rebels in those provinces could be bought. Sun Yat-Sen proposed that if the money was available he would be able to win over Yuan Shi-Kai's supporters and bring about his downfall, and then the stock of arms and ammunition would become redundant, and shall be made available to the Indians across the frontier. This grandiose plan appealed to Martin, and he thought that at last his dream of appearing on the Indian frontier with enough arms to raise an army of liberation would succeed.

M. N. Roy wrote in his Memoirs: "It was so very plausible from my point of view that I completely ignored its fantastic nature as far as Sun Yat-Sen was concerned. Many years later, having made myself more intelligently acquainted with the history of modern China and her numerous revolutions, I learned that Sun Yat-Sen disapproved of the Third revolution, because its leader, the Governor of Yunan, was a follower of the noted liberal-politician, Lian Chin-Chao."[2] Nevertheless, Naren left for China, to negotiate the deal.

From the day Naren landed at Nagasaki, he was under strict police surveillance. He, therefore, decided to travel to China by way of Korea and change his routes often to delude his chasers. The next afternoon, he went to the biggest Departmental Store. Even foreigners had to take off their shoes at the entrance in exchange for cloth shoes so that the dirt from streets did not spoil the spotless matting. Instead of returning to the main entrance to remove his shoes he went out by another door straight to the Railway Station. He wanted to get rid of the four police agents on his track.

The next morning he crossed over to Pusan and took the train for Seoul, but actually bought a ticket for Mukden. He wanted to switch off the main track at Seoul, and go to the port of Chimoolpo and travel across the Yellow Sea to Shanghaikwan or Tientsin. Rashbehari had informed him that an important leader of the Ghadr Party was living in the German concession there. To make sure that the police were no longer on the track, he decided to give another twist to his route. Instead of going as far as Shanghaikwan, he left the ship stealthily at Dairen, took the main train for Mukden and changed there for Peking. But although he had bought the ticket for Peking he left the through train at Shanghaikwan, stayed there overnight and took a local train to Tientsin.

At the Station platform he was accosted by a British policeman: "Good Morning, Mr. White . . . ." (Naren was in Japan in that name.) Naren tried to avoid and bypass him, but the policeman promptly fell in step and said: "Before you go to your destination, would you mind accompanying me for a few minutes." In his Memories, M. N. Roy describes the incident as follows: "I enquired where and why? 'To the Police Station; I am the Police Chief.' 'I had informed myself previously that the railway station was in the Russian Concession; and the German was just across the street in front. I made a desperate attempt: 'I am very tired after the journey and would rather go straight to a good hotel. Moreover, I believe we are not in British territory.' He became officious: 'That's all right. I know my business. Really, I may not detain you long. Come along.' "

"In the police station he asked me a few routine questions, and concluded by saying: 'I am afraid you shall have to spend the night here. We shall make you as comfortable as possible. . . . We are expecting some information from Japan.' Seeing that I was beaten, I hazarded, 'How did you know that I was coming?' He laughed and said: 'Oh, the Japanese Police is very efficient. Good night.' He was gone and I found myself behind heavy iron grilles."

The experience of being locked up like that was not new to Naren. Curiously enough, in that situation, he always went to sleep for hours. Breakfast came in the morning and the police chief soon thereafter. "Are you ready to accompany me to the Consulate?" Naren followed him. In

the car, the policeman said that he was going to be presented in the Consular Court. "On what charge?" Naren enquired. He shrugged his shoulders. "We are waiting for
the report." The Consul-General was an aristocratic looking old man—He looked sour, but spoke to him with polite-
ness. Why did Naren go to Japan? Why did he see in
Tokyo a secret agent of the notorious Rash Behari Bose?
What did he propose to do in future? Naren replied with
feigned contrition: "I wanted to go to England for study;
the war prevented it."[3] The Consul-General listened atten-
tively to his story and then asked the Police Chief: "Have
you received any further report from Japan?" The grim
reply was: "No, Sir, but it may come any time." The
British sense of justice saved Naren.

The policeman was furious. Out of the room he muttered
'the old fool'. Then he asked Naren where he wished to go.
"To a good hotel", Naren replied. "There is only one," he
said, " . . . but it is in the British Concession." Nonchalantly,
Naren reported that he wanted to go there; he was a British
subject. It was a fine hotel. Naren badly needed a hot bath
and a good meal. Immediately, thereafter, Naren obtained
a map of the city. In the afternoon, he went out in a rick-
shaw—to the Chinese part of the town, with the plan to go
to a point nearest to a small river. The German Concession
was just on the other side. But two other rickshaws followed
him.

It was getting dark; Naren got into a big shop and
loitered about for quite some time, until the police-watchers,
out of sheer boredom, went to the nearest tea shop. He
took the opportunity, slipped out by a side door to a narrow
lane and reached the river a few steps ahead. He took a
ferry boat and put a bit of silver in the boatman's palm.
The boatman pushed off leaving the other passengers behind. In a couple of minutes, he was in safety and the next
day he contacted the local German Consulate.

Martin then made a most difficult and hazardous trip to
Hankow and returned to Peking with a concrete agreement
and an accredited emissary of the Yunan leader to sell the
arms for five million dollars. But while admitting that the

final version of the plan was quite reliable and strategically sound, the German Ambassador regretted his inability to spend such a large sum of money. Thus this plan also failed; and Naren at last realised that the German promise to help an armed uprising in India "was a hoax, a veritable swindle".[4]

Having spent a year travelling through Malay, Indonesia, Indo-China, the Phillipines, Japan, Korea and China in fruitless search for arms, Naren finally landed in San Francisco in the summer of 1916.[5] It was during this journey through South-East Asia that Naren made a deep impression on the then nationalist revolutionaries of small Asian countries, like Sygman Rhea, Ho Chi Minh and others. Sygman Rhea, who was struggling to liberate Korea, told an Indian journalist later that in his early days, M. N. Roy made a deep impression on him. "Roy was a turbulent man struggling to liberate his country; his turbulence made a deep impression on me in my younger days."[6] The next morning after his arrival in U.S.A., the local newspaper carried the headline: "Mysterious Alien Reaches America—Famous Brahmin Revolutionary or Dangerous German Spy." Shortly after his arrival in the United States, Naren went to the nearby town of Palo Alto, the seat of the Stanford University and made the acquaintance of Dhangopal Mukherjee, younger brother of Dr. Jadugopal Mukherjee, to whom an intimation letter had already been sent informing of Naren's possible arrival, in advance. The same evening, Narendranath Bhattacharya adopted the name, Manabendra Nath Roy (M. N. Roy), "to wipe out the past, and begin a new man".[7]

NOTES AND REFERENCES

1 James Campbell Ker, *Political Trouble in India (1907-1917)*, pp. 282-83.
2 M. N. Roy's *Memoirs*, p. 7.
3 *Ibid.*: pp. 8-10.
4 *Ibid.*: p. 11.
5 *Ibid.*: p. 4.
6 Interview with P. N. Roy.
7 M N. Roy's *Memoirs*, p. 22.

# Epilogue

THE MILITANT NATIONALIST MOVEMENT THAT DEVELOPED IN Bengal at the turn of the century and climaxed in the Indo-German collaboration for armed insurrection in 1915 was built on one single motivation—to drive away the alien rulers. The movement was inspired by Vivekananda's ideal of building up a nation of heroes and on the idealism of the *sanyasis* preached by Bankim Chandra in his *Ananda Math*. This was in sharp contrast with the Moderate leaders in Congress whose objective was limited to larger participation of Indians in the Government of the country run by an alien power.

One of the major achievements of the terrorist-revolutionaries was the growth of a spirit of opposition, the spirit to defy the British rule. This spirit and the men who were involved in the movement subsequently strengthened the nationalist politics, particularly in Bengal. They formed the left wing in the Congress and articulated the demand for complete independence. The militant nationalist movement initiated by the Jugantar and Anushilan groups had blazed a new trail in Bengali politics and ushered in a spirit of aggressiveness and violence that has dominated Bengali political life for decades and whose influence can be traced even in contemporary times.

The extremist group of these early militants was led by Barin Ghosh who wanted to scare the British by indulging in "terrorist" activities, and failing to drive them away, at least to stir up the revolutionary spirit of the Bengalis. Barin's method obviously smacked of immaturity and romanticism, and as one of his compatriots, Purna Sen, said: "we had made many mistakes" because "we had no predecessors. We were pioneers".[1] Upen Banerjee, one of the accused in the Alipore Bomb Case, has described vividly in his remarkable memoirs, *Nirbasiter Atmakatha* (Memoirs of a Deportee), how childish and immature the whole plan was. What was there and what did survive was the high spirit of idealism and patriotism of these pioneers which inspired a whole host of new recruits to the revolutionary movement. Returning from the Andamans, where he was deported with others, Banerjee became a follower of M. N. Roy and a sympathiser of the communist movement when serving as the editor of the journal, *Atma Sakti*.

Among the early leaders of militant nationalist movement only Aurobindo had conceived of a concrete plan of action which he had communicated to Jatin Mukherjee in their very first meeting. But Aurobindo retired from active politics very early. The tension that developed between his brother, Barin, on the one hand, and Jatindranath Banerjee and Jatin Mukherjee on the other, both of whom were highly regarded by Aurobindo, was probably one of the reasons for his dissatisfaction and his subsequent retirement from active politics. As Aurobindo later told Nirvana Swami when the latter visited him in Pondicherry sometime in 1910 that he thought it was necessary for this country to build up better men first, and he had embarked on his spiritualist mission with that object.[2]

Jatin Mukherjee and Jatindranath Banerjee actively took up Aurobindo's plan for armed insurrection and Jatindranath Banerjee, who is regarded as Jatin Mukherjee's later political 'guru', was always available to Jatin Mukherjee for political advice. Even after Banerjee had retired into the life of a *sanyasi* in 1907, adopting the name, Niralamba Swami, Jatin Mukherjee sought his advice and acted only after the latter had given his consent. After the German plan had matured, Jatin Mukherjee went to Niralamba Swami at the latter's retreat at Brindaban and obtained his consent before going into active organisation.[3]

In contrast with most nationalist revolutionaries, Naren, even though inspired by the same idealism, was intensely a political revolutionary and always weighed the pros and cons of different political plans from a purely political standpoint, and without the help of gurus. He was his own master and by 1911 he was regarded as one of the politically most advanced in the group.[4] Naren's political ideas and adroitness and daring spirit attracted Jatin Mukherjee who later took him into close confidence. Unlike others, Naren was least religious although he often took the garb of a *sadhu*-seeking religious man as cover for his revolutionary activities. This garb of Naren had deluded not only the police but also many of his compatriots. Phani Chakravarty, one of his Changripota cousins and compatriot, who was close to Jatin Mukherjee, had described Naren as a *sadhu*-seeking religious man between 1911 and 1914 in his confessions to the police,[5] when Naren was at that period actively pursuing the plan for reorganising the revolutionaries and building up the organisation. After acquittal from the Howrah Gang Case, Jatin Mukherjee told his close associates to abstain from dacoities and other revolutionary actions and build up the organisational bases for the future.[6] It was in pursuance of that plan that Naren at times took up the garb of a *sadhu*-seeking religious man which confounded even many of his compatriots.

It was the German plan worked out by Naren that brought about a new situation and provided the *raison-d'etre* for the organisation of the Jugantar Party in the wake of the First World War. Although the plan for armed insurrection with German help did not mature in the end, the Government of India was seriously perturbed by the network of revolutionary organisations that was built up in this connection. Following unearthing of the conspiracy in 1915, a large number of revolutionaries were arrested and warrants of arrest issued against a larger number who escaped to different parts of the country and remained in hiding. The revolutionary activities culminating in the Indo-German plan for armed insurrection caused serious rethinking in the British Government to devise ways and means to prevent such activities. The Government appointed a Commission headed by Mr. Justice Rowlatt "to investigate into the revolutionary movement and recommend legislation that may be deemed necessary to suppress it", and the result was the passing of the Anarchical and Revolutionary Crimes Act of 1919 which provided for speedy trial of offences by a Special Court, which would meet in camera, and from which there could be no appeal. "It was urged by the Government that India might be well described as almost in a state of unarmed revolt, and the underground revolutionary movement, spreading over a wide region in India, was far from being rooted out altogether."[7]

The plan for armed insurrection with German help had appealed to Naren and he considered Jatin Mukherjee as the best person to provide the required overall leadership for the necessary unification of all political forces towards the implementation of the grandiose plan. He probably was conscious of his own limitation, partly also because of his rather uncompromising nature which at times made him unpopular among his fellow revolutionaries.[8] But even though an activist and a daring one at that, Naren evidently preferred the role of an adviser and to act under cover of a popular leader. This preference to combine the role of an adviser and an activist is evident in his character throughout his life. His initial success in such a role with Jatin Mukherjee prepared him for such roles in Mexico and also with Lenin in Moscow. His later break with the Communist International occurred when the post-Lenin Comintern leadership decided to curb his importance as the adviser-theoretician on colonial affairs. Returning to India in the 'thirties, M. N. Roy wanted to play a similar role with Jawaharlal Nehru and chose him as his leader after release from jail. When Sardar Patel and other rightist leaders of the Congress offered him high position if he agreed to become the leftist leader within the Congress against Nehru on the eve of the Faizpur session, M. N. Roy not only refused the offer but immediately informed Nehru of the conspiracy.[9] But the god that he chose evidently disowned him.

91

Whenever Naren conceived of an idea, even in his later life, and if that idea appealed to him, he always pursued it zealously despite all opposition, almost in an uncompromising manner. Although uncompromising in nature and one of the most daring of revolutionaries, Naren never took an action if it endangered the group and the plan itself. He always calculated the risks involved in every action before executing it and this also at times earned him unpopularity. One such case was the uncommitted Garbeta (Midnapore) dacoity for the looting of the cash of the Midnapore Zemindery Company shortly after the election of Jatin Mukherjee as the leader of the newly-formed revolutionary party, Jugantar, in late 1914. Many important leaders of Jugantar had gone there to commit the dacoity—which was to be the first after the formation of the united party—and Naren was chosen as the leader. Arriving at Garbeta, Naren decided against the dacoity because the chosen site of the looting was too close to the local Police Station. He also suspected while going to the local revolutionary's house when he had to pass by the Police Station that the police may have received advance information. Amar Krishna Ghosh, an important member of the group, told me that in fact the police had received information. One senior police officer called Ghosh after the group had left for Garbeta and advised him to send information to the group to put off the planned dacoity. Naren, however, on his own had already disbanded the group and asked them to return by two separate routes.[10] This angered some of the stalwarts of the Jugantar Party known to be daring adventurists.[11] Later, however, it was Naren who had to commit the first dacoity to raise funds which Jatin Mukherjee needed for the execution of the German plan. This was the sensational Garden Reach political dacoity which was planned and executed by Naren himself. This cool-headedness combined with courage and political adroitness which was also evident in his decisions endeared him to Jatin Mukherjee.

Thus, at the time of the proposed Indo-German collaboration for armed insurrection, Naren and Jatin Mukherjee needed each other. Jatin Mukherjee found in Naren the political man who could do the organisation, planning and execution of a master plan. Naren wanted Jatin Mukherjee because it was he who could provide the required prestige and personality to the leadership of the party for the implementation of his grandiose plan. When the Germans wanted a representative from the revolutionary group to go to Batavia for working out the details of the plan, it was, therefore, Naren who was chosen to go, which caused dissatisfaction among others. But Jatin Mukherjee decided to send Naren as he was the man who was best suited for the role and also because it was he who had conceived of the whole plan. Evidently, as Naren has later written in his Memoirs (as M. N. Roy), the Germans were not too sincere in their intention to support the Indian cause, and Naren left for America in the summer of 1916 a disappointed man.

When Naren finally landed in America he had nothing to return for immediately. Jatin Mukherjee had died, the organisation that had been built up was shattered and there was no prospect for an armed insurrection in the near future at least. Besides, he had second thoughts about the plan itself. He was now groping for new ideas; he was in fact trying to rethink and relearn political methods, about society and revolution, with a new mind, by casting off the old. The restless child[12] had become restless again for new knowledge and newer ideas. His adoption of a new name in the campus of the Stanford University was not merely to delude his chasers—he was conscious that it would not work for long. It was symbolic of his desire to live a new life, to remake himself.

His exposure to the world while in search of arms had brought him face to face with the political realities of other countries and provided him with an international view of things. This exposure to international political forces and his realisation of the inadequacy of the insurrectionist political method that he had been pursuing for the liberation of his country prepared him for his later transformation from a nationalist to an international socialist.

Naren began his life questing for freedom—freedom

which was essentially spiritual. In the wake of the anti-partition agitation, Naren's gradual transformation from spiritualism to revolutionary nationalism took shape. What remained of spiritualism in him following this transformation was his deep moorings in the concept of the *Brahman* as Cosmic Consciousness and His image of a detached, self-less spirit—a spirit that guided Naren throughout his life. It is this spirit of selfless detachment that distinguished Naren, and later M. N. Roy, from most other politicians. And it is this attitude of mind and the characteristic of the man that deprived him of those qualities which make a successful politician in modern times—the craving for personal power and leadership. As Roy himself wrote: "Success is the measure of greatness, and men greater than the successful great men are known to have preferred unpopularity to paying the prices of success."[13]

Although not religious in the popular sense of the term, Naren retained absolute faith in the ultimate goodness of nature. Hence he never became the frustrated man that many unsuccessful politicians were found to be. Perhaps this faith in the ultimate goodness of nature which flowed from his faith in *satchidananda*[14] was the basis of the humanist philosophy that he propounded later in his life. His stubborn optimism also grew out of this frame of mind.

Naren's pride about his Brahmanic tradition never left him, and it is from this attitude of mind that all his thinking and action emanated. In his *Memoirs,* M. N. Roy refers to his "Brahmanic tradition of intellectual aristocracy" with pride.[15] He elaborated this further to say, "My socialist conscience struggled hard to deny to myself the empirical truth that, while I felt at home in the company of a feudal aristocrat, the uncouth comrades never ceased to embarrass me".[16] "Concretely", M. N. Roy writes his Memoirs, "I felt that an aristocrat, intellectually emancipated from the prejudices of his class, might be a more disinterested and culturally more Dyonisian revolutionary than the most passionately class-conscious proletarian".[17]

Naren was one of the truest disciples of Sivnarain Swami; and the latter's teaching that 'Brahmanism devoid of its ritualism and superstitions could be a great heritage for India' made a deep mark in him. In his later life, as M. N. Roy, one of his chief missions of life was to rescue Indian society from the ills of ritualism, superstitions and obscurantism. He was a restless Brahmin in search of a Brahmanic haven on earth.

N O T E S  A N D  R E F E R E N C E S

1 My interview with Purna Sen.

2 My interview with Nirvan Swami.

3 My interview with Bhupendra Kumar Dutt.

4 Amar Krishna Ghosh said in his interview: "Narenda always thought about plans how to take the movement forward under the existing circumstances, and ceaselessly worked with that purpose in mind. He was a dynamic leader in contrast to others."

5 Phani Chakravarty's confessions made to the Police in Singapore in 1916, obtained from Government of India Archives, New Delhi.

6 Interview with Bhupendra Kumar Dutt.

7 R. C. Majumdar: *History of the Freedom Movement in India,* Vol. III, p. 3.

8 Bhupati Majumdar told me: Naren was uncompromising in respect of his political ideas and his ideas could not be influenced by closest friends.

9 As told to me by K. K. Sinha.

10 Interviews with Amar Krishna Ghosh and Nalini Kar.

11 Interview with Monoranjan Gupta.

12 Kali Prasad Banerjee told me during the interview: "I first met Narenda after our group (Faridpur group) accepted Jatinda as the leader in late 1914. I met him at the residence of Atul Krishna Ghosh after the Rodda loot. He was pacing up and down the room and was an embodiment of energy. He appeared to be a restless man, always wanting to do something."

13 M. N. Roy's *Memoirs,* p. 162.

14 Harikumar Chakravarty refers to a discussion between Laxman Sastri Joshi and M. N. Roy in later life and quotes Roy as saying "I want *Satchidananda".* Satchidananda, according to the Sanskrit dictionary, *Sabdakalpadruma,* is a synonym for *Brahman,* denoting a state of knowledge and delight in complete detachment.

15 M. N. Roy's *Memoirs,* p. 163.

16 *Ibid.* : p. 163-64.

17 *Ibid.* : p. 165.

# LITERATURE OF THE REVOLUTIONARIES

A short account of the books which were eagerly read by the nationalist revolutionaries is given here.

The first favourite was a book called *Jaliat Clive* (Clive, the Forgerer). As the title indicates, the object of the book was to depict that British rule in India was established by forgery and fraud.

Two other historical titles were *Maharaj Nanda Kumar,* and the *Life of Rana Pratap.* Life of Rana Pratap Singh was published in Calcutta in 1906 and dedicated to the student community of Bengal with the hope and desire that they would emulate the example of Rana Pratap in heroically adhering to the vow to fight for his motherland.

Closely following those three in popularity were *Sikher Balidan* and *Bhagawat Gita,* and the works of Bankim Chandra Chatterjee. The most celebrated of the works of Bankim Chandra and the one which appealed most strongly to the revolutionaries is the novel, *Ananda Math.*

## Ananda Math

*Ananda Math* exercised a great influence on the Bengali revolutionaries. Its author, Bankim Chandra Chatterjee was born in 1838 and studied in an English School. He graduated from the Hooghly College and passed Law from the Presidency College in Calcutta. He was one of the first graduates of the Calcutta University and was appointed a Deputy Magistrate.

By the time Bankim Chandra finished his College career the intellectual life in Calcutta had reached a glorious height. Bankim Chandra throbbed with an intellectual ferment. Bankim Chandra began to write novels and conduct a periodical entitled *Bangadarshan* in 1872. The magic charm of his pen soon resuscitated the Bengali language and imparted a unique life and vigour to it.

*Ananda Math* is a story of the *sanyasī* rebellion that took place from 1772 to 1774 when a famine swept over Bengal. *Sanyasi* is a religious mendicant and there were always hundreds of thousands of them roaming about everywhere in India. In the years mentioned a party of sepoys were sent against them with their leader Captain Thomas near Rangpur in North Bengal in January 1773. It was not till regular army operations were undertaken that these wandering mendicants could be gradually suppressed.

The novel describes the adventures and heroism of one of these bands of *sanyasis* who called themselves *santan* (children), that is children of the Motherland. Their headquarters were in the temple called *Ananda Math,* and they were initiated by taking a vow to renounce home and friends "till the Mother is saved, to give up riches and pleasures, to conquer their passions, to make over all their earnings to the Society, to fight for the true religion and never to flee from the battle-field". They were also required to give up distinctions of caste: "All the children belong to one caste; we do not make any distinction between Brahmins and Sudras in this great mission." The children greeted one another with the words *"Bande Mataram"* (Bow to the Mother).

Part of the initiation ceremony was to sing the Bande Mataram song, a song in praise of the Motherland. Those who were initiated gave up their own names, adopted *sanyasi* names, in the tradition of Hindu monks, such as Bhavananda, Satyananda and Jivananda.

Many ideas were afterwards taken from this novel by the leaders of Bengal revolutionary societies and the special vow taken by members of the Anushilan Samiti was practically the same as that of the children. The greeting, *Bande Mataram,* later became the chief slogan of the nationalist revolutionaries.

### Bande Mataram

*"I bow to thee, mother,*
*Richly-watered, richly-fruited,*
*Cool with the winds of the south,*
*Dark with the crops of harvests,*
*The mother!*

97

G

# THE RESTLESS BRAHMIN

*Her strands rejoicing in the glory of the moonlight,*
*Her lands clothed beautifully with her trees in flowering bloom,*
*Sweet of laughter, sweet of speech,*
*The mother, giver of boons, giver of bliss!*
*Terrible with the clamorous shout of seventy million throats,*
*And the sharpness of swords raised in twice seventy million hands,*
*Who sayeth to thee, Mother, that thou art weak?*
*Holder of multitudinous strength,*
*I bow to her who saves,*
*To her who drives from her the armies of her foemen,*
*The Mother!*

*Thou art knowledge, thou art conduct,*
*Thou our heart, thou our soul,*
*For thou art the life in our body,*
*In the arm thou art might, O mother,*
*In the heart, O mother, thou art love and faith.*
*It is thy image we raise in every temple.*
*For thou art Durga holding her ten weapons of war,*
*Kamala at play in the lotuses*
*And Speech, the goddess, giver of all love*
*To Thee I bow!*

*I bow to thee, goddess of wealth, pure and peerless,*
*Richly-watered, richly-fruited, the mother!*
*I bow to the mother*
*Dark-hued, candid*
*Sweetly smiling, jewelled and adorned,*
*The holder of wealth, the lady of plenty*
*The mother!"**

### Bhawani Mandir

This pamphlet, written by Aurobindo Ghosh sometime towards the latter part of 1904 and published without the au-

---

* This translation of Bande Mataram by Sri Aurobindo is taken from
Biman Behari Majumdar's *History of Political Thought*, Vol. I, Bengal,
pp. 419-20.

thor's name on it in 1905 played an important role to stir up young Bengalis. It explains the ideas underlying the revolutionary movement, particularly in the establishment of a sort of monastic retreat, or Ashram, as it is called, for teaching revolutionary work. It also supplies the meaning of many of the Hindu religious terms used in revolutionary literature.

As the author points out, *Bhawani* is the one of the manifestations of the goddess *Durga;* she was the tutelary goddess of Shivaji, the Maratha hero, and his celebrated sword was called after his *Bhawani.* Aurobindo Ghose, who wrote the pamphlet in the capital of an important Maratha State perhaps had this in mind in choosing the subject and the title especially in view of the close spiritual link between the Shivaji movement and the nationalist-terrorist movement in Bengal.

### *Bhawani Mandir*
#### OM NAMAS CHANDIKAYAI

A temple is to be erected and consecrated to Bhawani, the mother, among the hills. To all the children of the mother the call is sent forth to help in the sacred work.

#### WHO IS BHAWANI?

Who is Bhawani, the mother and why should we erect a temple to her?

#### BHAWANI IS THE INFINITE ENERGY

In the nonending revolutions of the world, as the wheel of the Eternal turns mightily in its courses, the Infinite Energy, which streams forth from the Eternal and sets the wheel to work, looms up in the vision of man in various aspects and infinite forms. Each aspect creates and marks an age: Sometimes she is love, sometimes she is knowledge, sometimes she is Renunciation, sometimes she is Pity. This Infinite Energy is Bhawani; She also is Durga; She is Kali; She is Radha, the Beloved; She is Lakshmi; She is our Mother and the Creatress of us all.

## THE RESTLESS BRAHMIN

### Bhawani is Shakti

In the present age, the Mother is manifested as the mother of strength. She is pure Shakti.

### The Whole World is Growing Full of the Mother as Shakti

Let us raise our eyes and cast them upon the world around us. Wherever we turn our gaze, huge masses of strength rise before our vision, tremendous, swift and inexorable forces, gigantic figures of energy, terrible sweeping columns of force. All is growing large and strong. The Shakti of war, the Shakti of wealth, the Shakti of Science are ten-fold more mighty and colossal, a hundred-fold more fierce, rapid and busy in their activity, a thousand-fold more prolific in resources, weapons and instruments than ever before in recorded history. Everywhere the Mother is at work; from Her mighty and shaping hands enormous forms of Rakhsasas, Asuras and Devas are leaping forth into the arena of the world. We have seen the slow but mighty rise of great empires of the West, we have seen the swift irresistible and impetuous bounding into the life of Japan. Some are *mlechha* (impure, foreign) Shaktis clouded in their strength, black or blood crimson with *tamas* or *rajas,* others are *Arya,* Shaktis, bathed in a pure flame of renunciation and utter self-sacrifice; but all are the Mother in Her new phase, remoulding, recreating. She is pouring her spirit into the old; she is whirling into life the new.

### We in India Fail in all Things for Want of Shakti

But in India the breath moves slowly, the afflatus is long, is coming. India, the ancient mother, is indeed striving to be reborn, striving with agony and tears, but she strives in vain. What ails her—she who is after all so vast and could be so strong? There is surely some enormous defect, something vital is wanting in us, nor is it difficult to lay our finger on the spot. We have all things else, but we are empty of strength and void of energy. We have abandoned *Shakti* and we are, therefore, abandoned by *Shakti*. The Mother is not in our hearts, or in our brains, or in our arms.

The wish to be reborn we have in abundance, there is no deficiency there. How many attempts have been made, how many movements have been begun, in religion, in society, in politics ! But the same fate has overtaken or is preparing to overtake them all. They flourish for a moment, then the impulse wanes, the fire dies out, and if they endure, it is only as shells, forms from which the Brahma has gone or in which it lies overpowered with *tamas* and inert. Our beginnings are mighty, but they have neither sequel nor fruit.

Now we are beginning in another direction; we have started a great industrial movement which is to enrich and regenerate an impoverished land. Untaught by experience, we do not perceive that this movement must go the way of all the others, unless we first seek the one essential things, unless we acquire strength.

## Our Knowledge is a Dead Thing for Want of Shakti

Is it knowledge that is wanting? We Indians, born and bred in a country where *jnana* (wisdom) has been stored and accumulated since the race began. We hear about the inherited gains of many thousands of years. Great giants of knowledge rise amongst us even today to add to the store. Our capacity has not shrunk, the edge of our intellect has not been dulled or blunted, its receptivity and flexibility are as varied as of old. But it is a dead knowledge, a burden under which we are bowed, a poison which is corroding us, rather than as it should be a staff to support our feet and a weapon in our hands; for this is the nature of all great things that when they are not used or are ill-used, they turn upon the hearer and destroy him.

Our knowledge then, weighed down with a heavy load of *tamas,* lies under the curse of impotence and inertia. We choose to fancy indeed now-a-days, that is, we acquire Science, all will be well. Let us first ask ourselves what we have done with the knowledge we already possess, or what have those who have already acquired Science been able to do for India. Imitative and incapable of initiative, we have striven to copy the methods of England, and we had not the strength; we would now copy the methods of the Japanese, a still more energetic people; are we likely to succeed any better? The mighty force of knowledge which European Science bestows is a weapon for the hands of a giant, it is the mace of Bhimsen (Bhima, the second of the Pandava brothers in Mahabharata); what can a weakling do with it but crush himself in the attempt to wield it?

## OUR BHAKTI CANNOT LIVE AND WORK FOR WANT OF SHAKTI

Is it love, enthusiasm, *Bhakti* (devotion) that is wanting? These are ingrained in the Indian nature, but in the absence of *Shakti* we cannot concentrate, we cannot direct, we cannot even preserve it. Bhakti is the leaping flame. *Shakti* is the fuel. If the fuel is scanty how long can the fire endure?

When the strong nature, enlightened by knowledge, disciplined and given a giant's strength by *Karma* (self-effort), lifts up in love and adoration to God, that is the Bhakti which endures and keeps the soul for ever united with the Divine. But the weak nature is too feeble to bear the impetus of so mighty a thing as perfect *Bhakti;* he is lifted up for a moment, then the flame soars up to Heaven, leaving him behind exhausted and even weaker than before. Every moment of any kind of which enthusiasm and adoration are the life must fail and soon burn itself out so long as the human material from which it proceeds is frail and light in substance.

## INDIA THEREFORE NEEDS SHAKTI ALONE

The deeper we look, the more we shall be convinced that one thing wanting, which we must strive to acquire before all others, is strength—strength physical, strength mental, strength moral, but above all strength spiritual which is the one inexhaustible and imperishable source of all the others. If we have strength everything else will be added to us easily and naturally. In the absence of strength we are like men in a dream who have hands but cannot seize or strike, who have feet but cannot run.

## INDIA, GROWN OLD AND DECREPIT IN WILL, HAS TO BE REBORN

Whenever we strive to do anything, after the first rush of enthusiasm is spent a paralysing helplessness seizes upon us. We often see in the cases of old men full of years and experience that the very excess of knowledge seems to have frozen their powers of action and their powers of will. When a great feeling or a great need overtakes them and it is necessary to carry out its promptings in action, they hesitate, ponder, discuss, make tentative efforts and abandon them or wait for the safest and easiest way to suggest itself, instead of taking the most direct; thus the time when it was possible and necessary to act passes away. One race has grown just such an old man with stores of knowledge, with ability to feel and desire, but paralysed by senile sluggishness, senile timidity, senile feebleness. If India is to survive, she must be made young again. Rushing and billowing streams of energy must be poured into her, her soul must become, as it was in the old times, like the surges, vast, puissant, calm and turbulent at will, an ocean of action or of force.

### INDIA CAN BE REBORN

Many of us, utterly overcome by *tamas,* the dark and heavy demon of inertia, are saying now-a-days that it is impossible; that India is decayed, bloodless and lifeless, too weak ever to recover; that our race is doomed to extinction. It is a foolish and idle saying. No man or nation need be weak unless he chooses, no man or nation need perish unless he deliberately chooses extinction.

### WHAT IS A NATION? THE SHAKTI OF ITS MILLIONS

For what is a nation? What is our mother-country? It is not a piece of earth, nor a figure of speech, nor a fiction of the mind. It is a mighty Shakti, composed of the Shaktis of all the millions of units that make up the nation, just as Bhawani Mahisha Mardini sprang into being from the Shaktis of all the millions of gods assembled in one mass of force and welded into unity.

103

# THE RESTLESS BRAHMIN

The Shakti we call India, Bhawani Bharati, is the living unity of the Shaktis of three hundred million people; but she is inactive, imprisoned in the magic circle of *tamas,* the self-indulgent inertia and ignorance of her sons. To get rid of *tamas* we have but to wake the Brahma within.

## IT IS OUR OWN CHOICE WHETHER WE CREATE A NATION OR PERISH

What is it that so many thousands of holy men. Sadhus and *Sanyasis* have preached to us silently by their lives? What was the message that radiated from the personality of Bhagwan Ramkrishna Paramhansa? What was it that formed the kernel of the eloquence with which the lion-like heart of Vivekananda sought to shake the world? It is this, that in every one of these three hundred millions of men, from the Raja on his throne to the coolie at his labour, from the Brahmin absorbed in his *sandhya* to the Pariah walking shunned of men, **GOD LIVETH.** We are all gods and creators, because the energy of God is within us and all life is creation; not only the making of new forms is creation, but preservation is creation, destruction itself is creation. It rests with us what we shall create; for we are not, unless we choose, puppets dominated by Fate and Maya; we are facets and manifestations of Almighty Power.

## INDIA MUST BE REBORN, BECAUSE HER REBIRTH IS DEMANDED BY THE FUTURE OF THE WORLD

India cannot perish, our race cannot become extinct, because among all the divisions of mankind it is to India that is reserved the highest and the most splendid destiny, the most essential to the future of the human race. It is she who must send forth from herself the future religion of the entire world, the Eternal religion which is to harmonise all religion, science and philosophies and make mankind one soul. In the sphere of morality, likewise, it is her mission to purge barbarism (mlecchahood) out of humanity and to *aryanise* the world. In order to do this, she must first re-aryanise herself.

It was to initiate this great work, the greatest and most

wonderful work ever given to a race, that Bhagwan Ramkrishna came and Vivekananda preached. If the work does not progress as it once promised to do it is because we have once again allowed the terrible cloud of *tamas* to settle down on our souls —fear, doubt, hesitation, sluggishness. We have taken some of us the Bhakti which poured forth from the one and the Jnana given us by the other, but from lack of Shakti, from the lack of Karma, we have not been able to make our Bhakti a living thing. May we yet remember that it was Kali, who is Bhawani, mother of strength whom Ramkrishna worshipped and with whom he became one.

But the destiny of India will not wait on the falterings and failings of individuals; the mother demands that men shall arise to institute her worship and make it universal.

### To Get Strength we Must Adore the Mother of Strength

Strength then and again strength and yet more strength is the need of our race. But if it is strength we desire, how shall we gain it if we do not adore the mother of strength? She demands worship not for Her own sake, but in order that She may help us and give Herself to us. This is no fantastic idea, no superstition but the ordinary law of the universe. The gods cannot, if they would, give themselves unasked. Even the Eternal comes not unaware upon men. Every devotee knows by experience that we must turn to Him and desire and adore Him before the Divine Spirit pours in its ineffable beauty and ecstacy upon the soul. What is true of the Eternal, is true also of Her who goes forth from Him.

### Religion the True Path

Those who, possessed with Western ideas, look askance at any return to the old sources of energy may well consider a few fundamental facts.

### The Example of Japan

I. There is no instance in history of a more marvellous and

sudden up-surging of strength in a nation than modern Japan.
All sorts of theories had been started to account for the uprising, but now intellectual Japanese are telling us what were
the fountains of that mighty awakening, the sources of that
inexhaustible strength. They were drawn from religion. It was
the Vedantic teachings of Oyomei and the recovery of Shintoism
with its worship of the national Shakti of Japan in the image
and person of the Mikado that enabled the little island empire
to wield the stupendous weapons of Western knowledge and
science as lightly and invincibly as Arjun wielded the Gandiv.

### INDIA'S GREATER NEED OF SPIRITUAL REGENERATION

II. India's need of drawing from the fountains of religion is
far greater than was ever Japan's, for the Japanese had only
to revitalise and perfect a strength that already existed. We
have to create strength where it did not exist before, we have
to change our natures, and become new men with new hearts,
to be born again. There is no scientific process, no machinery
for that. Strength can only be created by drawing it from the
internal and inexhaustible reservoirs of the Spirit, from that
Adya-Shakti of the Eternal which is the fountain of all new
existence. To be born again means nothing but to revive the
Brahma within us, and that is a spiritual process—no effort of
the body or the intellect can compass it.

### RELIGION THE PATH NATURAL TO THE NATIONAL MIND

III. All great awakenings in India, all her periods of mightiest
and most varied vigour have drawn their vitality from the
fountain-heads of some deep religious awakening. Wherever the
religious awakening has been complete and grand, the national
energy it has created has been gigantic and puissant; wherever
the religious movement has been narrow or incomplete, the
national movement has been broken, imperfect or temporary.
The persistence of this phenomenon is proof that it is ingrained
in the temperament of the race. If you try other and foreign
methods we shall either gain our end with tedious slowness,
painfully and imperfectly, or we shall not attain it at all. Why

abandon the plain way which God and the Mother have marked out for you, to choose faint and devious paths of your own treading?

### THE SPIRIT WITHIN IS THE TRUE SOURCE OF STRENGTH

IV. The Brahma within, the one and indivisible ocean of spiritual force is that from which all life, material and mental, is drawn. This is beginning to be as much recognised by leading Western thinkers as it was from the old days by the East. If it be so, then spiritual energy is the source of all other strength. There are the fathomless fountain-heads the deep and inexhaustible sources. The shallow surface springs are easier to reach, but they soon run dry. Why not then go deep instead of scratching the surface? The result will repay the labour.

### THREE THINGS NEEDFUL

We need three things answering to three fundamental laws.

### I. BHAKTI—THE TEMPLE OF THE MOTHER

We will, therefore, build a temple to the white Bhawani, the mother of strength, the Mother of India; and we will build it in a place far from the contamination of modern cities and as yet little trodden by man, in a high and pure air steeped in calm and energy. This temple will be the centre from which Her worship is to flow over the whole country; for there, worshipped among the hills, She will pass like fire into the brains and hearts of Her worshippers. This also is what the Mother has commanded.

### II. KARMA—A NEW ORDER OF BRAHMACHARINS

*Adoration will be dead and ineffective unless it is transmuted into Karma:* We will, therefore, have a *math* with a new Order of Karma-Yogins attached to the temple, men who have renounced all in order to work for the Mother. Some may, if they choose, be complete Sannyasins, most will be Brahmins who will return to the *grihasthasram* when their allotted work is finished, but all must accept renunciation.

## WHY? FOR TWO REASONS

(1) Because it is only in proportion as we put from us the preoccupation of bodily desires and interests, the sensual gratifications, lusts, longings, indolences of the material world, that we can return to the ocean of spiritual force within us.

(2) Because for the development of Shakti, entire concentration is necessary; the mind must be devoted entirely to its aim as a spear is hurled to its mark; if other cares and longings distract the mind, the spear will be carried out from its straight courses and miss the target. We need a nucleus of men in whom the Shakti is developed to its uttermost extent, in whom it fills every corner of the personality and overflows to fertilise the earth. These, having the fire of Bhawani in their hearts and brains, will go forth and carry the flame to every nook and cranny of our land.

## III. JNAN, THE GREAT MESSAGE

*Bhakti and Karma cannot be perfect and enduring unless they are based upon Jnana:* The Brahmacharins of the Order will, therefore, be taught to fill their souls with knowledge and base their work upon it as upon a rock. What shall be the basis of their knowledge? What but the great *so-aham*, the mighty formula of the Vedanta, the ancient gospel which has yet to reach the heart of the nation, the knowledge which when vivified by Karma and Bhakti delivers man out of all fear and all weakness.

## THE MESSAGE OF THE MOTHER

When, therefore, you ask who is Bhawani the mother, She herself answers you: "I am the Infinite Energy which streams forth from the Eternal in the world and Eternal in yourselves. I am the Mother of the Universe, the Mother of the Worlds, and for you who are children of the Sacred Land, Aryabhumi, made of her clay and reared by her sun and winds, I am *Bhawani Bharati*, Mother of India."

Then if you ask why we should erect a temple to Bhawani, the Mother, hear Her answer: "Because I have commanded it, and because by making a centre for the future religion you will be furthering the immediate will of the Eternal and storing up merit which will make you strong in this life and great in another. You will be helping to create a nation, to consolidate an age, to aryanise a world. And that nation is your own, that age is the age of yourselves and your children, that world is no fragments of land bounded by seas and hills, but the whole earth with her teeming millions."

Come then, hearken to the call of the Mother. She is already in our hearts waiting to manifest Herself, waiting to be worshipped,—inactive because the God in us is concealed by *tamas*, troubled by Her inactivity, sorrowful because Her children will not call on Her to help them. You who feel Her stirring within you, fling off the black veil of self, break down the imprisoning walls of indolence, help Her each as you feel impelled, with your bodies or with your intellect or with your speech or with your wealth or with your prayers and worship, each man according to his capacity. Draw not back, for against those who were called and heard Her not She may well be worth in the day of Her coming; but to those who help Her advent even a little, how radiant with beauty and kindness will be the face of their Mother!

The work and rules of the new Order of *Sanyasis* will be somewhat as follows:

## I. GENERAL RULES

(1) All who undertake the life of Brahmacharya for the Mother will have to vow themselves to Her service for four years, after which they will be free to continue the work on return to family life.

(2) All money received by them in the Mother's name will go to the Mother's Service. For themselves they will be allowed to receive shelter and their meals, when necessary, and nothing more.

(3) Whatever they may earn for themselves, e.g. by the publication of books, etc. they must give at least half of it to the service of the Mother.

(4) They will observe entire obedience to the Head of the Order and his one or two assistants in all things connected with the work or with their religious life.

(5) They will observe strictly the discipline and rules of *achar* and purity, bodily and mental, prescribed by the Heads of the Order.

(6) They will be given periods for rest or for religious improvement during which they will stop at the *math,* but the greater part of the year they will spend in work outside. This rule will apply to all except the few necessary for the service of the Temple and those required for the central direction of the work.

(7) There will be no gradations of rank among the workers, and none must seek for distinction or mere personal fame but practice strength and self-effacement.

## II. WORK FOR THE PEOPLE

(8) Their chief work will be that of mass instruction and help to the poor and ignorant.

(9) This they will strive to effect in various ways:

- (*i*) Lectures and demonstrations suited to an un-educated intelligence.
- (*ii*) Classes and nightly schools.
- (*iii*) Religious teachings.
- (*iv*) Nursing the sick.
- (*v*) Conducting works of charity.
- (*vi*) Whatever other good work their hands may find to do and the Order approves.

## III. WORK FOR THE MIDDLE CLASS

(10) They will undertake, according as they may be directed, various works of public utility in the big towns and elsewhere, connected especially with the education and religious life and

instruction of the middle classes, as well as with other public needs.

## IV. Work with the Wealthy Classes

(11) They will approach the zamindars, landholders and rich men generally, and endeavour:

(*i*) To promote sympathy between the zamindars and the peasants and heal all discords.

(*ii*) To create the link of a single and living religious spirit and a common passion for one great ideal between all classes.

(*iii*) To turn the minds of rich men to works of public beneficence and charity to those in their neighbourhood independent of the hope of reward and official distinction.

## V. General Work for the Country

(12) As soon as funds permit, some will be sent to foreign countries to study lucrative arts and manufactures.

(13) They will be as Sanyasis during their period of study, never losing hold of their habits of purity and self-abnegation.

(14) On their return they will establish with the aid of the Order, factories and workshops, still living the life of Sanyasis and devoting all their profits to the sending of more and more such students to foreign countries.

(15) Others will be sent to travel through various countries on foot, inspiring by their lives, behaviour and conversation, sympathy and love for the Indian people in the European nations and preparing the way for their acceptance of Aryan ideals.

After the erection and consecration of the Temple, the development of the work of the Order will be pushed on as rapidly as possible or as the support and sympathy of the public allows. With the blessing of the Mother this will not fail us.

### *Bhagavat Gita* and *Chandi*

Two religious books that found a prominent place in the literatures for the revolutionaries were the *Bhagavat Gita* and *Chandi*.

# THE RESTLESS BRAHMIN

The passage in the *Gita* which appealed most to the revolutionaries is the one which relates how the family of the Pandavas, with Arjuna at their head, is drawn up in battle against their cousins, the Kauravas. Arjuna, seeing his relatives arrayed against him, declares to Sri Krishna, who acts as his charioteer, that for nothing in the world will he slay his kinsmen even though they are prepared to kill him.

Sri Krishna tells Arjuna: "These bodies appertaining to the embodied self which is eternal, indestructible and indefinable, are said to be perishable; therefore engage in battle, O descendant of Bharata! He who thinks the self to be the Killer and he who thinks it to be killed, both know nothing. It kills not, is not killed. It is not born, nor does it ever die, nor, having existed, does it cease to exist. Unborn, everlasting, unchangeable, and primeval, it is not killed when the body is killed."

"Oh Son of Pritha! How can that man who knows it thus to be indestructible, everlasting, unborn and inexhaustible, how and whom can he kill, whom can he cause to be killed? As a man, casting off old clothes puts on new ones, so the self casting off old bodies, goes to new ones. Weapons do not divide it into pieces; fire does not burn it; waters do not moisten it; the wind does not dry it up. It is not divisible; it is not combustible; it is not to be moistened; it is not to be dried up. It is everlasting, all pervading, stable, firm and eternal. It is said to be unperceived, to be unthinkable, to be unchangeable."

"Therefore, knowing it to be so, you ought not to grieve. But even if you think that it is constantly born, and constantly dies, still, oh, you of mighty arms! you ought not to grieve thus. For to one that is born, death is certain; and to one that dies, birth is certain. Therefore about this unavoidable thing you ought not to grieve."

"Happy those Kshattriyas, Oh son of Pritha! to whom such a battle as this comes of itself—an open door to heaven! . . . If slain, you will attain heaven; victorious you will possess the earth."

Another passage which had great influence is the following: "He whose heart is not agitated in the midst of calamities, he who has no longing for pleasures, and from whom affection, fear and wrath have departed, is called a sage of steady mind.

112

His mind is steady, who being without attachments anywhere, feels no exultation and no aversion on encountering agreeable and disagreeable things."

The motto printed on the front page of *Jugantar* was also taken from Gita and reads as follows:

"When righteousness decays, Oh son of Bharata and unrighteousness flourishes, then I manifest myself. For the protection of the good, for the destruction of evil-doers, for the establishment of righteousness, I am reborn from age to age."

## *Chandi*

The book called *Chandi* is named after one of the epithets of the goddess *Durga* regarded as the destroyer of the demon *Chanda*. It relates how the gods, driven from their kingdom by the demons, created the goddess *Kali*, or *Adya Shakti* (primordial energy), a manifestation of the goddess *Durga*, to destroy the demons.

*Durga* has many manifestations. As the destroyer of demons she takes the form of *Kali*, and in this form she is sometimes called *Chandi*. The destruction of the demons is a regular metaphor in the literatures of the revolutionaries, the gods being the people of India and the demons, the English—and this accounted for the popularity of the books.

## *Bartaman Rananiti*

If the real meaning of this worship of the goddess of power, by whatever name—Kali, Shakti, Chandi or Bhawani—she may be known, were in any doubt, the doubt is entirely removed by this book. It was published in October 1907, by Abinash Chandra Bhattacharji, the friend, or as they preferred to call it for the purposes of the Manicktolla Conspiracy trial, the servant of Arabindo Ghose. This book was the principal revolutionary text-book; 394 copies were found in the Manicktolla Garden, and it was, as the issue register showed, one of the most popular books in the Dacca Anushilan Samiti library.

The title *Bartaman Rananiti* means "The Modern Art of War", but before going on to deal with military subjects the author reprints, as Chapter I of his book, an article which ap-

H

peared in the *Yugantar* newspaper in October 1906, entitled "War is the order of creation". After explaining that destruction is but creation in another form, the writer proceeds: "Destruction is natural and war is, therefore, also natural. When any part of the body is rotten it should be cut off with the help of surgical instruments, otherwise the gangrenous wound would expand and cause destruction to the body. Vice, persecution, dependence are but gangrenous sores in the body of the nation. War is inevitable when oppression cannot be stopped by any other means whatsoever, when the leprosy of slavery corrupts the blood of the body of the nation and robs it of its vitality. It is for this reason that Sri Krishna, god himself, acted as charioteer, holding the reins in his hands at the battle of Kurukshetra. It is for this reason that the god Ram Chandra planned the destruction of Ravan. It is for this that Chandī, inspired with the prowess of 33 crores of gods, appeared to kill the Daityas, and for this reason the incarnation of Kali in this Kali age, 'Kali holding two swords to destroy the Mlechhas', has passed into a saying of the Shastras."

The writer then discusses the rapid rise of Japan, and says: "This remarkable development is but the result of unflagging, and disinterested work." Hence Okakura has said: "Until the moment we shook it off, the same lethargy lay upon us which now lies upon China and India .... Religion could not soothe, not cure, the suffering of the wounded soul. But to-day Japan has been cured of her disease. Japan is now, therefore, not only the land of beautiful flowers and pictures of fair women, but also the Pithabhumi (place of pilgrimage) of the goddess of war."

Karma (or action) is the way to salvation and wealth, and it is to establish this Karma that the Hindus have set up the worship of Shakti. The new India, the worshipper of Shakti must not forget this principle of Karma. Action is wanted; fame is the reward of action, but the price of fame is very high. The sage Kamalakanta, wandering about in the market of the world, came to the Shop of Fame. "I Saw", he said, "darkness in the shop". I called the shopkeeper but no answer came. I heard only great cries striking terror into the hearts of all. In a faint light I read on the signboard at the door:

### Shop of Fame

Things sold—eternal fame
Price—Life

To attain to national fame five things are needful, religious faith, food, wealth, men and a warlike spirit. There is no want of faith or food or men in India; the remaining two things must be acquired. Swadeshi and boycott will bring wealth, while time, pointing to the English rifle, says "See, the warlike spirit in the artificer of the European palace; acquire the warlike spirit". The warrior's weapons are intelligence and physical strength, and strength of arms is necessary to demolish the rule of evil and to establish a kingdom of righteousness.

"We Indians are disarmed under the orders of the King. The foreign King, being in fear of his life lest his subjects, driven mad with oppression, should strike him on the head, has disarmed all the subjects of this country. The English employ the Sikhs, the Marathas and the Rajputs as soldiers, and teach them a little of the military art, but the intelligent Bengalis and the Brahmins of Poona are not even allowed to use a long stick. For who can say that the all-destroying arm will not in the twinkling of an eye demolish the British Kingdom? Because the King, in fear of his life, has passed laws contrary to religion, will therefore eight crores of Bengalis, more than twenty crores of Marathas and countless other warlike nations remain like beasts? True, we may not have opportunities of learning military manoeuvres and drill openly and in a lawful way. If, however, the Bengalis take this system of instruction into their own hands, they can, through self-exertion, become experts in horsemanship, and acquire courage, strength of arm, power of endurance and other heroic qualities, and they can master all the underlying principles of the science of war in the country by study and by preaching. If the Bengalis can do so much through diligence, they will never feel the want merely of arms. This book is published to lay the foundation of this new system of instruction. If, as a result of it, even one of the fetters drops off from the red lotus foot of the captive mother, her wretched son will consider himself fortunate."

The remainder of the book deals with the weapons of war, the organisation of armies, and tactics, particularly the tactics of guerilla warfare which is described as "the mode of fighting adopted by a nation, which is weak, disarmed and oppressed by conquerors, but resolved to break the bondage of slavery". Great stress is laid on the importance of the intellect in war. "Hence it was that the Japanese, though weaker and smaller in stature than the Russians, were more expert in war. Hence it was that 60,000 Boer peasants kept *lakhs* of British soldiers under their feet for three years. Hence it is that the British do not enlist the Bengalis or the Brahmins of Poona as soldiers."

In the last chapter the writer asks: "How can a weak and disarmed nation fight against armed and trained soldiers?", and replies, "The answer is very simple. There are many instances in the world's history which show that it is not impossible for a conquered people to gain victory. A nation may be disarmed and in the power of others. But if the people are firmly determined to drink the nectar of liberty, and if they accept death as desirable, then God will make them heroes. Regular fighting is then possible for them, because:

(1) Being inspired with patriotism, the native troops desert the side of the foreign king and join the heroes.

(2) The mountain tribes become excited by the greedy and fiery tongue of revolution and rush to the battle-field.

(3) The strength of the youths of a country being applied to irregular warfare, they gradually become fearless and expert in sword-play. Irregular fighting is therefore a test for them. Facing dangers constantly for the good of the country, they attain heroic qualities, such as courage, strength, presence of mind, etc.

(4) During the long period of anarchy and collision, people increase in number and they venture to accumulate wealth and arms.

(5) In a long protracted war even the enemy suffer. Many soldiers are destroyed, and commerce, taxes and other means of obtaining money being stopped, famine appears

in their own country, and other ruling powers take advantage of the occasion to harass them. In these circumstances who will not venture to defeat such worn-out foes? People perceive that two or more defeats will completely crush the oppressor, and they come in bands under the flag of the revolutionists, and the door of the treasury is flung open for the country's sake. Then with a swadeshi Government in power, agriculture and commerce will flourish again."

In October 1907, Arabindo Ghose's paper, the *Bande Mataram* published an appreciative notice of this book, remarking that it showed the new trend of the National mind, and that no doubt it would be eagerly sought after. "It is perfectly true", says the writer, "that no practical use can be made of its contents at the present moment; but the will and desire of thousands creates its own field, and when the spirit of a nation demands any sphere of activity material events are shaped by that demand in ways that at the time seem to be the wild dreams of an unbridled imagination".

### Mukti Kon Pathe?

This book, the title of which means "Which Way Lies Salvation?", is in four parts, and is simply a reprint of articles from the *Yugantar* newspaper. It also was a text-book both for the Manicktolla Garden group and for the Anushilan Samiti, and it is of importance as indicating the objects of the training that went on in both institutions, and the programme which the leaders adopted for the collection of men, money and arms.

For example, in Part II it is stated that the Bengalis are at a disadvantage in the way of muscular development. That is to be made good by training, so far as training can do so. There must be greater muscular development, but if the time at their disposal is not sufficient to secure such development, there is consolation in the thought that not much muscle is required to kill a European with a revolver or a rifle, or kill many Europeans with a Maxim gun. It does not take much strength to pull a trigger; even a Bengali can do that.

In another article, under the heading "Revolution" and the sub-heading "Building up public opinion", the means are stated as follows:

(1) Newspapers.
(2) Music (i.e. Songs, etc).
(3) Literature.
(4) Secret meetings and associations

Regarding No. (4) the writer says:

"Secret societies are necessary since it is impossible to talk of freedom openly because of bayonets and guns. If one wants to talk of freedom publicly he must necessarily do so in a roundabout way. It is precisely for this reason that a secret place is necessary where people may discuss 'What is truth'? without having recourse to hypocrisy. But it must be a place which the tyrant cannot see. The Russian revolutionists used to meet at dead of night in secret places to discuss what they ought to do, and they still do so. It is precisely this state of things which has been described by Bankim Babu in his *Ananda Math*. In the dead of night the sanyasis used to collect weapons for freedom in the dense forest." ... "When revolution is absolutely necessary for the sake of freedom it must be preached by all possible means. All means, great or small, important or unimportant, should be adopted."

In an article in Part IV the collection of arms is discussed, and the writer says that if firm determination be there arms come of themselves. "A nation yearning for freedom does not shrink even, if it be necessary, from collecting money by theft and dacoity. So, in the matter of collecting arms, the power of discriminating between right and wrong is gone. Everything is sacrificed at the feet of the goddess of liberty." There are three ways of obtaining arms:

(*i*) By preparing weapons silently in some secret place. In this way bombs are prepared by the Russian nihilists. Indians will be sent to foreign countries to learn the art of making weapons. On their return to India they will manufacture cannons, guns, etc. with the help of enthusiastic youths.

(*ii*) By importing weapons of all kinds from foreign countries.

(*iii*) Through the assistance of Native Soldiers. The native Army serves under the tyrannical King only to earn a livelihood. But they are human beings, and "when the revolutionists explain to them the misery and wretchedness of the country, they swell the bands of revolutionists at the proper time, taking with them the arms given to them by the King".... "It is because soldiers may thus be made to understand the situation that the present English King of India does not allow the clever Bengali to enter the army."

The reference made above to the collection of money by so-called political dacoities is elaborated in another article, in which it is explained that at first the work of preaching should be managed with the money obtained by begging or as a free gift. Secret preachers begin secretly to form bands in all directions at home and abroad. Much money is not needed for this purpose. If the work has not passed its infancy, the expenses can be met by subscriptions, etc. But if the work advances so far that we are compelled to collect much money it becomes impossible to depend on the money that is given willingly; money should then be exacted from society by the application of force . . . . If the revolution is being brought about for the welfare of society, then it is perfectly just to collect money from society for the purpose. It is admitted that theft and dacoity are crimes because they violate the principle of the good of society. But the "political dacoit" is aiming at the good of society; "so no sin but rather virtue attaches to the destruction of this small good for the sake of some higher good. Therefore, if revolutionists extort money from the misery or luxurious wealthy members of society by the application of force, their conduct is perfectly just."

The last stage is the robbery of Government treasuries. This also is justified because, from the moment the kingly power tramples upon the welfare of the subjects, the king may be regarded as a robber from whom it is perfectly right to snatch away his stolen money, in order "to defray the expenses of establishing the future kingly power".

# THE PRESS

## *Jugantar*

The first and most influential of the revolutionary papers of Calcutta was the *Yugantar* (New Era) started in 1906 by Barindra Kumar Ghose and Abinash Chandra Bhattacharji, members of the Manicktolla Conspiracy and Bhupendra Nath Dutt, the brother of Swami Vivekananda. Before being prosecuted the journal received on 7th June 1907, a warning from the Government of Bengal in respect of an article which appeared in the issue of 2nd June. The warning had no effect, and the issue of June 16th contained two articles entitled "Away with Fear", and "The Medicine of the Big Stick" for which Bhupendra Nath Dutta, as editor, was prosecuted. He admitted full responsibility for the articles and was convicted by Mr. Kingsford on 24th July 1907, and sentenced to one year's rigorous imprisonment; the press was ordered to be confiscated as an instrument used in the commission of the offence. On appeal the conviction and sentence were upheld, but the order of confiscation was set aside by the High Court on the ground that the press could not be so regarded.

A prosecution was, therefore, instituted against Abinash Chandra Bhattacharji as manager for the paper, and Basanta Kumar Bhattacharji, as printer and publisher, in respect of articles in the issue dated 30th July and 5th and 12th August 1907. Abinash was acquitted, as it was not proved that he sold the paper, and Basanta was convicted on 2nd September and sentenced to two years' rigorous imprisonment and a fine of Rs. 1,000. In the course of his judgment Mr. Kingsford remarked: "The tone of the paper as exhibited in the articles which are the subject matter of the present case has become greatly more inflammatory than before, and in convicting the accused Basanta of the offence charged, I think proper to award him a punishment of enhanced severity."

This also had no effect, and a third prosecution had to be

undertaken on an article entitled, "Hindu Heroism in the Punjab", published in the issue of 14th December of 1907. Baikunta Nath Acharjya, who had declared himself printer and publisher on 30th October 1907, was convicted on 16th January 1908, and sentenced to two years' rigorous imprisonment and a fine of Rs. 1,000. In the judgment in this case Mr. Kingsford remarked: "There can be no question as regards the seditious nature of the article; it is addressed primarily to the Sikh soldiers serving under the British Government, and it is an attempt to incite them to mutiny by putting forward a series of false, scurrilous and malicious charges against that Government."

"The prisoner was in Court on the occasion of a previous trial of the publisher of the *Yugantar*, and when he became the publisher on 30th October he must have been well aware of the nature of the newspaper and of the fact that the editor had been sentenced to one year's imprisonment under Section 124A, on the 24th July 1907, and the printer and publisher in respect of a subsequent offence under the same Section to two years' imprisonment and fine of Rs. 1,000 on the 2nd September 1907. There can be no doubt that the prisoner has published a series of seditious articles in pursuance of a settled plan of action. He says he is ignorant of their authorship; whether or not this is the truth, he is at any rate responsible for the fact that they have appeared in print. Under the circumstances I see no reason why I should refrain from imposing the severe penalty which the nature of the prisoner's offence demands.

"I need only add that the history of the *Yugantar* during the last few months exhibits the impotence of Government to deal with this class of publication under the existing law. In the interests of good Government and good order the paper ought long ago to have been suppressed. It is difficult to measure the harm which is likely to result from such an article as that charged, when it is translated and circulated, as presumably it is intended to be, amongst those to whom it is ostensibly addressed. And while the law remains in its present state, there is little reason to doubt that the party of disorder will, on the guarantee of a sufficient indemnity, procure another catspaw to take the prisoner's place."

This anticipation was fulfilled, and a fourth prosecution had to be instituted in respect of an article, "The Englishman's Despotism" in the issue dated 4th April 1908. Phanindra Nath Mitter, who had declared himself printer and publisher on the 4th March was convicted on 26th May and sentenced to rigorous imprisonment for one year and eleven months and a fine of Rs. 1,000. The Presidency Magistrate, on this occasion Mr. Thornhill, said in his judgment: "The article complained of speaks for itself. It is clearly seditious, and in my opinion no person, however extreme, could come to any other conclusion. Other articles, ten in number, from the issues of the 7th March, 11th April, 18th April and 2nd May of this year, have been put in by the prosecution to show the seditious character of this newspaper. They are all of a similar type and can leave no doubt in one's mind that the paper is run with the deliberate intention of stirring up strife and exciting disaffection towards Government."

The same Phanindra Nath Mitter was prosecuted a second time as printer and publisher for three articles which appeared in the issue of 9th May 1908. He was committed for trial to the High Court, and on 22nd July was convicted and sentenced to rigorous imprisonment for three years.

Again a new printer and publisher was found for the paper, named Barindra Nath Banerji. In the issue dated 30th May 1908 an article appeared entitled, "The Bengali's Bomb", in praise of bomb-throwers in general and the heroes of Muzaffarpur in particular. The printer and publisher was prosecuted for this article and committed to the High Court; on the 14th August. He was convicted and sentenced to rigorous imprisonment for three years.

In the meantime, on 8th June 1908, the Newspaper (Incitements to Offences) Act (VII of 1908) was passed. It provided for the forfeiture of presses in which newspapers containing incitements to murder, or to any offence under the Explosive Substances Act, 1908, or to any act of violence, were printed. This brought the *Yugantar,* as a newspaper, to an end, but the defect in the Act, that it applied only to newspapers, was at once noticed by the *Yugantar* gang who thereafter issued their revolutionary appeals in the form of leaflets.

Another prosecution connected with the *Yugantar* arose out

of a disturbance which took place on 7th August 1907, when the office of the paper was being searched. A crowd of students and others collected at the door, and Sailendra Nath Bose, an employee in the *Yugantar* office came out and informed the crowd that the premises were his and they could do what they pleased. Two European inspectors of police were assaulted with sticks in attempting to move the crowd on, and in consequence Sailendra Nath Bose and a student of the Ripon College named Jyotish Chandra Roy were convicted on the 26th August by Mr. Kingsford, and sentenced to rigorous imprisonment for three months and one month respectively.

## *Yugantar* [*Selections*]

That the *Yugantar* was revolutionary from the commencement, though it was not at first taken seriously, is apparent from the following extracts from the issue dated 17th June 1906:

"The foreigners manage by artifice to obtain and take away the wealth of the country and everything substantial in it, and throw the Indians, reduced by them to skeletons, into the horried jaws of famine, pestilence and poverty. On the one hand inactivity, lifelessness, impotence, scarcity and famine have gained a permanent footing in the land. Is this to be called peace? Or a revolution is an infinitely better thing than the peace under which mortality is fast rising in India. If even fifty millions of men disappeared from India in an attempt at deliverance, would even that not be preferable to death in impotency and peace? Why should he who was born a man and of a man die like a worm? Has the Almighty provided no means of deliverance for him who cannot prove himself a man and act as such in his life? He has. IF YOU CANNOT PROVE YOURSELF A MAN IN LIFE PLAY THE MAN IN DEATH. Foreigners have come and decided how you are to life. BUT HOW YOU ARE TO DIE DEPENDS ENTIRELY UPON YOURSELF. Others have meddled in your mode of living, but no one can meddle in your mode of dying. The right of deciding how you are to die is your own. If you cannot show yourself a man in life, show yourself one in death—that is the teaching of the times."

## THE RESTLESS BRAHMIN

The following passage from an article which appeared on the 3rd March 1907, is one of many advocating the use of physical force and justifying bloodshed as a religious duty.

"The laws of the English are based on their brute force. If we want to liberate ourselves from those laws, it is brute force that it is necessary for us to accumulate. It is there, then, that the right course of action now lies for us. It will not do to go against the law for all time. *Swarajya* will never be established if in the humiliation of truth is sought protection for self. In our country must be re-enacted what has happened in other countries. There is no other door of admission into life but death."

"You will inquire how, being weak, we can enter on a trial of strength with the powerful English."

"Be not afraid. Not very many listened to the young Mazzini on the day when, wounded to his heart's core by the sufferings and poverty of Italy, he firmly received to free his country from bondage. But to-day Italy has expiated her own sin and has washed away in human blood the blackness of her stigma. Oh, sons of Bengal, worshippers of *Shakti,* will you be averse from that? Under the stress of plague and famine, lakhs and lakhs of people are dying every year in the country. And are not ten thousand sons of Bengal prepared to embrace death to avenge the humiliation of their fatherland? The number of Englishmen in the entire country is not more than a lakh and a half. And what is the number of English officials in each district? With a firm resolve you can bring English rule to an end in a single day. The time has come to make the Englishman understand that enjoyment of the sweets of dominion in the country of another, after wrongfully taking possession of it, will not be permitted to continue for ever. Let him now fully realise that the life of a thief who steals the property of others is no longer an easy one in this country. Begin yielding up a life for a life. Dedicate your life as an offering at the temple of liberty. Without bloodshed the worship of the goddess will not be accomplished."

The following is from the article, "Away with Fear", which appeared on 16th June 1907, and formed the subject of the first prosecution:

124

"In the course of conversation a respected *pandit* said the other day that this vast British Empire was a huge sham; that it was a house without a foundation or a garland strung without a thread; that though it glittered and looked so nice with its crimson hue, a slight pull or a little push would bring it down to fragments. That it does not fall is due simply to our foolishness. The tide of oppression has passed over us for century and century. Subjection for a thousand years has so bewildered us with fear that we cannot muster up enough courage even to come out of the privacy of our houses to see who is sitting to-day as king on the vacant throne. We see the high diadem from a distance and utter our prayers and take the name of God. Our king, too, seeing the opportunity, is aggravating our internal confusion by sometimes wielding the sceptre and some times smiling a forced smile. He and we have never become intimately acquainted with each other. A close look at the face of a ghost dispels all fear of it."

After looking at it from a distance for so long we, too, have at last come to suspect that the hands and feet of the ghost are not really so strong as its face is hideous; that the bugbear is not really so large as we have supposed it to be. What we ought to do now most of all, therefore, is to give a little push to the bugbear and see what happens. In the Punjab scarcely was the bugbear touched with a finger when it leapt and jumped, mostly from fear and partly also from anger.

What we want now is a number of men, who will take the lead in giving a push and thus encourage the masses and infuse hope in the minds of those who are almost dead with fear and dread. It will not do to form a company with those who are stiff with fear. Mere words will not convince such men. They must be shown by deeds done before their eyes that the work is not impossible exactly to the extent that they think it to be, and that the arms of the English are not so long as to grasp India and keep it within their grasp against our wish.

What is wanted, therefore, is a number of workers who will renounce every wordly thing and break off every wordly tie and plunge into the sea of duty; who will understand everything themselves and then make others understand; who will die themselves and deliver others from the fear of death; who will have neither home, nor son nor wife but will have only their Mother, the country of their birth, green with crops and well-watered. Will there not be found one in the whole of Bengal who is ready to respond to the Mother's call?

Once fear is dispelled the work will become easy and all the brag of the English will be of no avail.

The other article in the same issue on "The medicine of the big stick" contained the following:

"In Bengal we have cried ourselves hoarse during the last two years, and sent up the price of paper in the buzaar by using up quires upon quires in submitting petitions couched in the most correct and elegant language. But as the result of all this we have been fortunate enough to get nothing but thrusts of *lathis,* and partitioned Bengal remains parted. But in the Punjab a hue and cry was raised as soon as the water rate was enhanced. The period of making representations and submitting petitions did not last more than two weeks. The people then applied the remedy which is always applied to fools. There were a few heads broken and a few houses were burnt down, and the authorities gave up the idea of enhancing the water-rate. The Colonisation Act, too, became inoperative. How wonderful is the remedy! The Kabuli medicine is indeed the best of medicines."

The establishment of revolutionary secret societies is described in the following extract from the issue of 15th July 1907. It was not a mere academic discussion, for the heading of the article is "Shall we be able?"

"First the revolutionaries have to establish their own party all over the country. The centre (Central Association) of the revolutionary party has to be placed in the Capital City or in some other important place. Different branch Associations of the centre (Central Association) have to be established in other important places in the country; and in those branch Associations the common aim and method of work of the Associations are followed. These central and branch Associations silently and secretly do their own work in unison. Whether it be the branch Associations or the central Association, all of course, make, each in its own way, various preparations for a revolution, such as the formation of public opinion, collection of arms, collection of money, etc. but in everything they do they have to advance very secretly, keeping themselves outside the ken of the sovereign power. The sovereign power never quietly brooks preparations for its destruction. It tries its best to nip the tree of revolution in the bud. The party trying to secure independence has, therefore, to adopt various artifices in order to evade the eagle eye of the sovereign power."

"In this manner the necessity for a revolution has to be explained in various ways to the common people. The object of educating common people in this fashion is that at the time of real war with the sovereign power they will, instead of opposing, render help in various ways. Herein lies the strength of the following of the revolutionaries. By educating people in this manner, while the strength of the following revolutionaries increases that of the sovereign power decreases. If the true nature of the oppressor is painted in bright colours for the common people, and they are shown the oppression he commits can be brought to an end, then a desire to break the strong chain of subjection is created in their hearts also. There are various ways of educating people in this fashion. We shall mention only one or two. The sacred cry for independence must be raised from that direction from which it will be easiest to capture the public mind. The mind of man can be very quickly captured by means of newspapers, books, *jatra* (operatic performances), *kathakatha* (singing and narrating spirited poetry), etc. If therefore, the *mantra* (formula) of independence is popularised by these means, men's hearts very soon advance towards the field of action."

The *Yugantar* was naturally very strongly anti-British, as exemplified in this passage from the issue of 30th November 1907.

"To-day the Bengalis alone of all the Indians have understood that the Westerners are a set of fierce and blood-thirsty beasts of prey. They are a nation completely devoid of mercy, righteousness, conscience and manly virtues. They do not want the world to be made happy. They do not want righteousness in the world. They want to live for themselves only. They want everything for themselves to eat. They want to fill their coffers with all the treasures of all the nations of the world. They want all the inhabitants of the world to lay everything that they possess at their feet and become their slaves. The Bengalis have understood this, and are consequently trying to dispel the illusion. The Bengali is to-day making all India appreciate his own sterling divine qualities. This is why that avaricious, bloodthirsty nation is going about with open mouth and baring its fearful teeth to devour the Bengalis."

The article of 14th December 1907, on "Hindu Heroism in the Punjab", which formed the subject of the third prosecution of the *Yugantar,* was a very long one, consisting mainly of variations on the following theme:

"In the middle of the 18th (19th) century, in seeking to measure strength with the highly powerful Sikh race on the field of battle, even the soldiers of the English race, who now brag of the strength of their sword, but are averse to fighting and are strong through the help of the swords of the Sikh and the Gurkha, were compelled to flee like a flock of sheep. The sharp whipping of the battle of Chillianwalla the barbarous English are not even yet able to forget. The battlefields of Mudki, etc., still continue to float before the eyes of the people of India as so many proofs of English defeat. If the Punjabi heroes of the land of the five rivers, released from the spell (which is now on them), again step forward to battle for the defence of king and Brahmins in India, the drunken drowsy eyes of this Western race will at once look out for a way of escape, flinging far off the sword of whose power the English brag in the pride of unreal strength. A country cannot be ruled by cannon and rifles; manliness and heroism too are wanted. In how many battles have the English, so far, been victorious? Yet the inhabitants of the Punjab, like gods under a curse, do not even now revive the memories of the past and step forward to defend their country.... Nevertheless, Bengalis, consider this— how long will a handful of cowardly English remain in India if the Sikh nation again takes its stand as it did in the days when Lord Gough and others, in their bovine ignorance of the art of war, were taught a lesson at Chillianwalla."

In an article published on 2nd May 1908, on the subject of the Mutiny of 1857, which is described as "the first Indian war of independence", the writer says:

"Is it possible that the fire which was kindled fifty years ago has been altogether extinguished within so short a time? Is there no one who has kept some smouldering embers of that fire to burn the race of mlechhas? Has the flame of the fire, which has in all ages destroyed demons and monsters, been put out altogether? No, it cannot be. It may be that the fire has become invisible to ordinary sight, but the power latent in it is present all the same. That power can never be put down. It lies hidden in every atom, and its embers will burst out into a full blaze as soon as there is a favourable wind. Hence it cannot be said that the entire Indian nation has been enervated by servitude, as some would suppose. It is impossible for any nation to sink into the mire of subjection within so short a period as fifty years. The men who appeared in the arena the other day with clashing swords and thundering roars may be silent and quiet now, but the spirit which animated them is not yet dead."

The following are extracts from the article on "The Bengali's Bomb" in respect of which the paper was prosecuted for the sixth time:

"Bengali boys have learnt to make bombs, but they have not yet learnt to throw them well. It is because they are yet unable to take proper aim and hit the mark that in the Muzaffarpur accident they killed persons other than him whom they intended to kill. It is only because their hands were not trained and their heads not sufficiently cool that two innocent ladies have had to die.... It is beyond the vision of the secret spies of the *feringhi sirkar* to see where, in some solitary room in the kitchen, brothers, sisters, mothers and daughters together are making and can make bombs. Even the extensive machinery and factories of England have to own themselves beaten by the way in which the Bengali can manufacture bombs, guns, and cartridges. Let the unostentatious preparations for this great revolution be silently made and collected in every house. A handful of policemen and English soldiers will not be able to find them out. They will not be able to keep in check this extensive preparation for a great *Kurukshetra* by obstructing it. The inclination to make this preparation is due to the spirit of the age; it is a law of nature; it is the unobstructed awakening of the instinct of self-preservation of a sleeping race, persecuted, despised, and trampled under foot for a long time. Two or four boys have been arrested to-day. Al-

129

I

though Hem Chandra, Ullaskar and others will never more be united with us in the field of action—we know indeed that they will never escape from the grim jaws of the English—thousands and thousands of Hem Chandras and Ullaskars have come up again and are standing in front. Hence there is no reason to despair. The soil of India is ever fertile with the blood of heroes."

The same issue contained an article on "The Traitor's Expiation", an attack upon detectives and spies, which included the following:

"The enemy is trying to increase the number of traitors by bribes. They have made detectives even of high Government servants by holding out to them the temptation of money. We know all this. They are trying to gather information by sending about low class men as spies. In the bomb case at Alipur a barber is now giving his deposition as a spy. It is said that this barber followed Barindranath and others to almost every place. Such are the spies that are engaged, and they are trying to have all the young men who seek independence arrested. The country has become eager for their expiation. The public is showing great eagerness to know how these traitors will be detected and punished. This general eagerness will, we believe, soon take the form of action. And the indomitable spirit of revenge will continue to be terribly gratified by the traitor's blood. Once the national fire is roused it will be impossible for the antagonist to stand against it. Such wrath is never quicked until it has destroyed the antagonist's *gotra* (clan), *gosthi* (kindred) and *bansha* (family), and this wrath will doubtless reduce all to ashes, both the great offenders and those who are wrongly suspected. The time of expiation is at hand."

The Worship of *Shakti* (Power) was also discussed in the same number, in an article which included the following passage:

"Some of the Mother's votaries have been hitherto worshipping her in secret, and now they are revealing themselves slowly. This has caused a flutter among the race of monsters who are trying hard to thwart the noble enterprise of these true sons of India. But let us warn those cat-eyed fellows not to disturb the Mother's worship. The Mother is thirsty and is pointing out to her sons the only thing that can quench that thirst. Nothing less than human blood and decapitated human heads will satisfy her. Let her sons, therefore, worship her with these offerings, and let them not shrink even from sacrificing their lives to procure them. On the day on which the Mother is worshipped in this way in every village, on that day will the people of India be inspired with a divine spirit and the crown of independence will fall into their hands."

### *Sandhya*

Another paper closely connected with the *Yugantar,* and for a time printed at the same press, was the *Sandhya.* The title of the paper means "Twilight", and the point of it may be found in a remark made in the paper in September 1907, warning the English that after the passing of the *Sandhya* comes nightfall when the squaring of accounts with the *Feringhi* will begin. In August 1907, proceedings were taken against it; the manager Saroda Brahmo Bandhab Upadhyaya and the printer and publisher Hari Charan Das on 3rd September. While the case was still pending the editor died, and on 18th November the cases against the others were withdrawn as they explained that they had been entirely under the influence of the deceased, admitted that the articles charged were both scurrilous and seditious, and tendered an apology to the Government of Bengal.

### *Sandhya* [*Selections*]

A few extracts will illustrate the style of this paper. In an article published on the 13th April 1907, the *Sandhya* justified its abuse of the English in the following manner:

"The *Feringhi* has brought the printing press to this country, and it is he who has taught us the art of writing newspapers. In a word, the press, the paper, the pen, the post-office, the telegraph, everything belongs to the *Feringhi.* The newspapers written by the *Feringhi* are our guides. We simply avail ourselves of the opportunity thus given, and say a few words, but the *Feringhi* is the gainer all round. If now we make bold to speak out the truth, the law of sedition is sought to be brought into play to make us pay some more money. For, when a prosecution is started, the *Feringhi* Barrister must be employed, and must be paid handsomely. O what an admirable business instinct is this of the *Feringhi*! The *Feringhi* knows how to pick out gold even from an ash-pit. The *Feringhi* will say that we write many things in our paper only to create disaffection against their administration. But we have never asked anybody to extend his patronage to us. Yet our paper commands a sale, such a sale that we can hardly cope with the demand. We said once, and we repeat, O *Feringhi,* that in a country where even the internal spirits are sometimes worshipped, nothing but abusive language applied to you finds a market. Can you tell why this should be so? In reply we say that it is owing to your pettiness. O *Feringhi,* when you used to 'plunder treasuries and kill rhinoceroses', as the saying goes, when you were not a mean stealer of *lotas,* then such abuse did not find favour with the people of this country. You are now, as we said above, a thief who steals *lotas* and, therefore, you get what the petty thief must expect to get, nothing but reproaches. By partitioning Bengal you have gained a few posts and the means of draining the country by your administration, and no more. For this petty gain, for this worn-out *lota,* you have maddened and mortified the people of Bengal. Where, then, should calumnies about you be welcomed by the public if not in this country?"

On 29th April 1907, the paper began to advise the preparation of bombs.

"Let us all come forward now and unite to establish posts in every town and village. It will not do to stock these posts with lathis only. Fireworks will have to be laid in. If the *Feringhis* do not grant passes for guns, small bombs will have to be kept. Knowledge of the method of preparing bombs is necessary. One's own jurisdiction, one's own home will have to be protected with the aid of these fireworks, of these bombs."

The same subject was taken up again on 6th May 1907:

"There is one respect in which we are not ready yet. The *Feringhis* have taken away our guns from us and attack us with guns themselves. But even that is being provided for. Handbombs are being prepared of a kind which will beat your bullets hollow. We shall see how far the police muster courage then to commit oppression." . . ."Come now, brethren, let us make a move for the protection of our own and our rights.

But mere words will not avail. Without the *lathi* and the bomb the *Feringhi* will not be brought to his senses and will not care for you in the least."

The usual religious touch was added in another article in the same issue:

"It is a matter for great rejoicing that an excellent kind of bomb is being manufactured. This bomb is called *Kali Mai's boma* (the bomb of Mother Kali). It is being experimented on and if it comes out of the test successfully it must be kept in every house. This bomb is so light that one can walk with it in one's hand. It has not to be set fire to; it explodes with a loud noise and shakes the earth if it is thrown on the ground with some little force. People are frightened at this kind of talk, but why? Whence have you learnt the slavery which teaches that you cannot form a band for self-defence, while the non-official *Feringhis* can combine to form volunteer forces? A son is wanted from every family who must practise the virtues of the *Kshatriya* (Warrior). Let them play with *Kali Mai's boma*."

Again on 14th May 1907, the same point was pressed further:

"Abundant supplies should also be laid in of bows and arrows and of that *Kali Mai's boma* (Mother Kali's Bomb) of ours. It has not to be set fire to; it has simply to be thrown with a little force or dropped from a height among a band of *gundas* (rascals). As soon as it is thrown you hear a sharp sound, and ten to twenty men are brought down. It entails no cost to prepare this *Kali Mai's boma,* and it does not require to be stored in large quantities. These bombs can be prepared according as they are required."

The following extract is from an article which appeared in the *Sandhya*, dated 21st August 1907, one of those for which the paper was prosecuted:

"Most merciful is the *Feringhi*.
It is by his grace that our beard grows.
And that we eat sweet potatoes in winter."

"Thanks to the *Feringhi's* rules the pot is now sucked empty by him and wails are heard in every house in fruitful India. Thanks to his kindness our very bones are overgrown with grass. Every year the *Feringhi* drains away 25 crores of our money. Where then should plague and famine be if not in our country? It is those who have not enough to eat, sufficient clothing to cover themselves with, and comfortable beds to lie on, that fall victims to plague. It is in quarters inhabited by the poor that the plague makes desolating ravages. Has any one of you ever seen plague breaks out in Chowringhee? The plague is a disease to which the poor are peculiarly liable. Plague means poverty and we are dying of plague. Pestilence is for us, for we have no food in our stomachs; foreigners are snatching away morsels of food from our mouths. When the *Feringhi* had no food in his country he, too, used to die like us. Now that he has carried away by force the goddess of fortune, he is blessed with plenty. That is why the plague that used to afflict the *Feringhi* now sits on our shoulders. Strictly considered, it is the *Feringhi* who has brought plague into our country; in fact the *Feringhi* is our plague." After some remarks on the theory that plague is carried by rats the writer proceeds: "But the people of the country have far other notions of the cause of plague. They realise that it is the *Feringhi* rat who has brought plague into the country by robbing it of its wealth and food-grains. They realise that this rat is the root of plague. That is why they have set the trap of boycott to catch this rat, and now they see that, caught in this trap, the *Feringhi* is chewing fried rice; seeing this they shout with delight '*Bande Mataram*'."

### Bande Mataram

The *Bande Mataram* was a daily paper in English started in November 1906, by Arabindo Ghose and a few friends. The *Yugantar* was the paper for the masses; it was written in fluent colloquial Bengali; the circulation, which was about 7,000 in 1907, rapidly rose to a very much higher figure. The *Bande Mataram* was intended to appeal to a more educated class of readers, but it was closely connected with the *Yugantar*. *Bande Mataram* occasionally republished articles from its vernacular contemporary. One of these, and some of the editor's own writing got it into trouble, and a prosecution was started at the end of July 1907, in respect of an original article, "Politics for Indians" which appeared on 27th and 28th June, and the republication on 26th July of articles from the *Yugantar*. The latter appeared in the *Bande Mataram* under the heading *Yugantar* Case; articles on which action was taken, and occupied almost the whole page of the paper. The defence was that these articles formed part of a substantially true report of the proceedings of a court, but as a matter of fact only a few of them were exhibited in the *Yugantar* Case. The court accordingly held that "this was not a case where a mere sample of the venomous utterances of a vernacular paper was placed in good faith before the reader in order to give him an insight into the manners and ways of thought prevailing in that description of newspaper; the whole mass of seditious writings collected by the prosecution was republished under cloak of repeating the proceedings of a Court of Justice but with the actual intention of bringing the Government into hatred and contempt". The article "Politics for Indians" was also held to be seditious, the magistrate remarking: "To say that the Government has become a Government of Evil Spirits, is to say that the country is ruled by Evil Spirits; and it is against the Government that the calumny which follows is directed."

Discussing the evidence that Arabindo was the editor the magistrate observed: "This evidence is to the effect that Arabindo is a shareholder in the paper, that he took the chair at a preliminary meeting held in October, the minutes of which show that he and Bepin Chandra Pal were appointed joint editors that a notice was printed in the issue of the paper of 12th December to the effect that Arabindo was the editor, that this was followed on 17th December by another notice which announced that Bepin Chandra Pal had terminated his connection with the paper, that Arabindo was in Calcutta from April to July, and was attending at the *Bande Mataram* office, that his name was entered at the head of the list of the editorial staff in the pay register for January, February and March, which entries were subsequently erased, and that he received a sum of Rs. 50 in payment for service in July." The defence was that Arabindo was not the editor, but was employed on the staff and contributed to the editorial columns; that in fact there

135

was no editor but an editorial staff which was jointly responsible.

Owing mainly to the refusal of Bepin Chandra Pal to give evidence, for which he was afterwards convicted and sentenced to six months' imprisonment, the case against Arabindo Ghose failed. The manager, Hemendra Nath Bagchi, was also acquitted, as there was no evidence that he distributed the paper nor any presumption that he was aware of its contents. The printer and publisher only, Apurba Krishna Bose, was convicted on 23rd September 1907, and sentenced to rigorous imprisonment for three months, and his appeal was dismissed by the High Court in November.

A second prosecution was instituted in respect of an editorial headed "New Conditions" which appeared in the issue dated 30th April 1908, the day of the first successful revolutionary bomb outrage. The printer only, Bishnupada Sen, was prosecuted, but owing to his illness the case did not come on for hearing for some months. Meantime an article headed "Traitor in the Camp" appeared in the paper on the 14th September 1908. It was in praise of Kanai Lal Dutt who murdered Norendra Nath Gossain, the approver in the Manicktolla Conspiracy Case, and this time proceedings were taken under the Newspapers (Incitement to Offences) Act. The press was declared forfeit in November 1908, and on appeal to the High Court the Magistrate's order was upheld in December. The paper then ceased to appear, and the printer, Bishnupada Sen, recovered sufficiently from his illness to appear in Court on the 11th January and plead for leniency on this ground. The case was not pressed by the prosecution and he was warned and discharged.

## Bande Mataram [Selections]

The following is an extract from the article in the *Bande Mataram* on "Politics for Indians", in respect of which the first prosecution was undertaken:

"Mr. Morley has said that we cannot work the machinery of our Government for a week if England generously walks out of our country. While this supposition is not conceivable in the nature of man, did it not strike Mr. Morley that if, instead of walking out the English were by force driven out of India, the Government will go on perhaps better than before, for the simple reason that the exercise of power and organisation necessary to drive out so organised an enemy will in the struggle that would ensue teach us to arrange our own affairs sufficiently well."

Among the *Yugantar* articles re-published in the paper and included in the same prosecution was the following from the *Yugantar* of 5th May 1907:

"But it is useless to talk to you Englishmen in this strain. You are not a man, you are a demon, you are an "asura". Otherwise our Surendranath would not have talked all this nonsense to your representative near the battlefield of Jamalpore. You are surely a demon, or otherwise you would not on the one hand have converted the millions of educated Indians into lambs and, on the other, would not have induced thousands of Musalmans in Eastern Bengal to forget themselves and engage in a quarrel with their brothers. Your Minto and Hare are dangerous people who have no equal in the art of demoniac duplicity. Who calls you a tiger? Who calls you the British Lion? There are no tigers or lions in your country which contains only moles, jackles and dogs. In childhood we read only of these animals in your books and to-day in the field of politics, too, we are being acquainted with the self-same animals."

The article headed "New Conditions" suggests that the writer knew what was being attempted at Muzaffarpur. He says:

"An immense and incalculable revolution is at hand and its instruments must be themselves immense in their aspiration, uncalculating in their self-immolation. A sacrifice, of which the mightiest Yajna of old can only be a feeble type and far-off shadow, has to be instituted and the victims of that sacrifice are ourselves, our lives, our property, our hopes, our ambitions, all that is personal and not of God, all that is devoted to our own service and taken from the service of the country." Then, after a reference to the disruption of the Indian National Congress at Surat in December 1907, he concludes: "The disappearance of the old Congress announces the end of the preparatory stage of the movement, the beginning of a clash of forces whose first full shock will produce chaos. The fair hope of an orderly and peaceful evolution of self-government, which the first energies of the new movement had fostered are gone for ever. Revolution, bare and grim, is preparing her battle-field, moving down the centres of order which were evolving a new cosmos, and building up the materials of a gigantic downfall and a mighty new creation. We could have wished it otherwise, but God's will be done."

The following passages are taken from the article, "Traitor in the Camp" which led to the confiscation of the Press:

"From Jaychand to Oomichand is a far cry, but the political history of our country for all those long centuries of indelible shame can be summarised and accounted for in the four short words—'Traitor in the camp'." . . . . "And the no less singular feature of this ghastly thing is that through all these countless years it is always the person at whose instance he turned traitor who has punished the miserable miscreant, but the country could never find a single son to rise and avenge her on the hated monster by smiting him to the ground. Now for the time the current is turned. For the very first time a cause has produced a votary who has willingly sacrificed his life to visit on its betrayer his merited doom. Kanai has killed Norendra. No more shall the wretch of an Indian who kisses away the heads of his comrades reckon himself safe from the avenging hand. The first of the avengers' History shall write of Kanai. And from the moment he fired the fatal shot the spaces of his country's heaven have been ringing with the echo of the voice 'Beware of the Traitor's fate'."

### Karmayogin

Arabindo Ghose's next journalistic venture was a weekly magazine called the *Karmayogin* (The Devotee of Action) started in June 1909. In the issue dated 25th December 1909, a letter headed "To my Countrymen" appeared over the signature of Arabindo Ghose. It was considered very objectionable and proceedings were instituted, but no attempt was made to arrest Arabindo till the beginning of April 1910, when he was found to have taken refuge in Pondicherry. The printer, Monmohan Nath Ghose, was prosecuted, and in June he was convicted and sentenced to six months' rigorous imprisonment under Section 124A, Indian Penal Code. He appealed to the High Court, and after lengthy arguments and discussions between the bench and the bar the conviction and sentence were set aside in October. Arabindo Ghose, however, did not return to Calcutta, and the magazine came to an end.

*Index*

# INDEX

# INDEX